"Hilarious."
—*New York Post*

"When it comes to memoirs, things don't get more heartfelt than this. And when it comes to storytelling, few could match the humor, passion, and humanity of these pages."
—*New York Journal of Books*

"Moving and perceptive and of great value for any creative artist or would-be artist . . . [Smith] talks unflinchingly of the temptations and compromises that face any aspiring artist and keeps coming back to the same messages of courage and comfort: Trust yourself. Do what you know is right. He calls it 'tough shit,' but it's more like tough love—funny, compassionate, and wise."
—*Kirkus Reviews*

"*Tough Sh*t* seems easy to recommend to any hard-core Smith fan. . . . Overall, this autobiography is a low risk for a high-reward investment."
—Geeknative.com

"His utter awe and thankfulness for his own success shines through to that nerdy kid from Jersey whose only dream was to do what he loved: make movies."
—NerdMentality.com

"It's a breezy, entertaining, crass-but-funny read."
—*The A.V. Club*

"Forget Broadway—Kevin Smith's self-help book will show you how to succeed without really trying."
—*Penthouse*

"Kevin Smith is nicer than he lets on, thinner than he thinks, and smarter than almost anyone in the room. He has today's world—and tomorrow's—running for cover."
—Mitch Albom

"Kevin Smith is a force of nature: He makes movies, he writes books and stuff, he talks, and then he talks some more. Maybe he's less of a force of nature and more of a spreading cloud of secondhand weed smoke that is slowly infiltrating every medium available to us. Kevin Smith is the haze that binds us all."

—Marc Maron

• • •

A writer, comedian, podcaster, and film director, Kevin Smith has written and directed numerous films, including *Clerks*, *Chasing Amy*, *Dogma*, and *Red State*; authored *Silent Bob Speaks*, *Shootin' the Sh*t with Kevin Smith*, and the *New York Times* bestsellers *My Boring-Ass Life* and *Batman: Cacophony*. He can be heard daily at Smodcast.com, a vast network of podcasts. His body and belongings may be found in Los Angeles, but it's a well-known fact that Smith actually lives on Twitter: @ThatKevinSmith.

• • •

Tough Sh*t

Life Advice from a
Fat, Lazy Slob Who Did Good

KEVIN SMITH

GOTHAM BOOKS

GOTHAM BOOKS
Published by the Penguin Group
Penguin Group (USA) Inc., 375 Hudson Street, New York, New York 10014, USA ·
Penguin Group (Canada), 90 Eglinton Avenue East, Suite 700, Toronto, Ontario
M4P 2Y3, Canada (a division of Pearson Penguin Canada Inc.) · Penguin Books Ltd,
80 Strand, London WC2R 0RL, England · Penguin Ireland, 25 St Stephen's Green,
Dublin 2, Ireland (a division of Penguin Books Ltd) · Penguin Group (Australia),
707 Collins Street, Melbourne, Victoria 3008, Australia (a division of Pearson Aus-
tralia Group Pty Ltd) · Penguin Books India Pvt Ltd, 11 Community Centre,
Panchsheel Park, New Delhi–110 017, India · Penguin Group (NZ), 67 Apollo
Drive, Rosedale, Auckland 0632, New Zealand (a division of Pearson New Zealand
Ltd) · Penguin Books, Rosebank Office Park, 181 Jan Smuts Avenue, Parktown
North 2193, South Africa · Penguin China, B7 Jaiming Center, 27 East Third Ring
Road North, Chaoyang District, Beijing 100020, China

Penguin Books Ltd, Registered Offices:
80 Strand, London WC2R 0RL, England

Published by Gotham Books, a member of Penguin Group (USA) Inc.

Previously published as a Gotham Books hardcover

First trade paperback printing, February 2013
5 7 9 10 8 6 4

Gotham Books and the skyscraper logo
are trademarks of Penguin Group (USA) Inc.

Copyright © 2012 by Kevin Smith

THE LIBRARY OF CONGRESS HAS CATALOGUED THE HARDCOVER
EDITION AS FOLLOWS:

Smith, Kevin, 1970-
Tough sh*t : life advice from a fat, lazy slob who did good / Kevin Smith.
p. cm.
ISBN 978-1-59240-689-0 (hardcover)   978-1-59240-744-6 (paperback)
1. Smith, Kevin, 1970-   2. Motion picture producers and directors—
United States—Biography.   3. Screenwriters—United States—
Biography.   I. Title.   II. Title: Tough shit.
PN1998.3.S5864A3 2012
791.4302'33092—dc23
[B]   2011047663

Printed in the United States of America

*Penguin is committed to publishing works of quality and integrity.
In that spirit, we are proud to offer this book to our readers;
however, the story, the experiences, and the words
are the author's alone.*

Like its author, this book is dedicated to Jen Schwalbach—the gorgeous mother of my child, the seductive temptress who keeps me faithful, and the friend I've always had the most fun with. My best friend, even.

Also quite like its author, this book is additionally dedicated to Jen Schwalbach's asshole.

Everything above also applies here, obviously, except the "mother of my child" part: Referencing my kid and my wife's brown-eye in the same sentiment might come off as *crude* or something.

(And have a heart: Please don't go telling my kid you read in her old man's book that she's some kinda Butt-Baby. She's gonna have a hard enough time as it is being Silent Bob's kid—the daughter of the "Too Fat to Fly" guy.

Also: Please don't tell my daughter I dedicated the book to her mother's sphincter. That'd be weird.)

CONTENTS

CHAPTER ONE

Let's Get This Shit Started!

I am a product of Don Smith's balls.

That's important to establish and acknowledge right off the bat, not only because it makes what I've accomplished in life seem even cooler, but also because Dad's balls have been, to my way of thinking, too rarely celebrated. Unless you count whatever attention Mom threw their way, I don't feel they've gotten their proper due for their part in what became of me. And she's certainly never hailed his nuts in print, so this right here is a real coup for the Smiths of 21 Jackson Street, Highlands, New Jersey. Though if you could ask my father, he'd likely admit that while having his balls in print is flattering, having his balls in my mother's mouth was way better.

People need to be regularly reminded that they began as cum. Not to diminish or cut 'em down to size—quite the contrary: I tell people they were cum once as a gesture of my awe at their very existence and to pat 'em on the back. There are no losers in life because every one of us who is born is a *huge* fucking winner.

Chew on this: When I was in film school, there was this specious statistic floating around stating there were more film school students than law school students. That was one massive pool of wannabes who'd have to bottleneck into a souvenir teacup full of opportunities waiting on the other end of the rainbow. Breaking into the movie business? Don't worry, Cap'n Solo; even C-3PO can't calculate those odds. Might as well try to navigate an asteroid field.

And that's what people congratulate you for: the fact that you—simple, normal you—cracked the code and got into the club. You get to see your name in lights and somehow *that's* impressive. I remind these people that my most impressive accomplishment—like theirs (and yours, dear reader)—is that we beat out *billions* of tough competitors for the job of a lifetime. Motherfuck being the Sundance flavor of the month; being the sole product of that careless cumshot my old man somehow kept in my mom is akin to beating the Kurgan and becoming the Highlander. There can be only one (aside from twins, triplets, quadruplets, and quints—the monsters and freaks of the baby world). Whenever someone tells me I'm fat, I tell 'em I wasn't always: Apparently, at one point in my life, I was fit enough to out-swim a legion of sperm. And now, like any past-their-prime athlete, I'm enjoying the good life: I hoisted my Cup already, so at this point, fuck off and lemme enjoy bacon and brownies (maybe even together).

You beat sock drawers full of dead cum that didn't have

a chance coming out the gate. The odds that you wound up in an egg instead of a paper towel? Astronomically against you.

Some might have considered Don Smith's balls mere mute witnesses in my father's masturbatory war against his dick, but not Grace Schultz. My mom saw the potential in my dad's balls. She didn't see her unborn children in his eyes, she saw them outlined in the nooks and crannies of his testicles. And of all the wads my father busted during his too-short stay in this sector of the galaxy, I wound up in the moneyshot. And more than that, I didn't get burned to virtual death like Anakin Skywalker on the lava shores of Mom's nethers. I am, you am . . . we *all* am the best of billions.

Chuckle if you must, but all this jism talk is the important first step on the road to self-actualization. Fuck Tony Robbins; you wanna *really* inspire people? Remind them they've already beaten the odds, so the existence that follows is merely a victory lap to do with as they please. You're a big, fat bucket of win when you begin this crapshoot life; no need to pressure yourself to do much more than use your time here as the wind-down to the only real contest that'll ever matter: you vs. a billion other applicants.

Don Smith was a good guy and I owe him and my mom, Grace, everything I have. But I owe Dad maybe a little bit more. My whole life has been a reaction to his life, really—but mercifully not in any textbook manner that ever called for rebellion. For starters, I am literally a reaction (the nut) to his action (sexing Mom). Also: He worked at the U.S. Postal Service and hated it like a jihadist. Most people hate their jobs, true, but my old man despised his in an Ahab-and-Moby (or Eminem-and-Moby) kinda way. He never said, "Go into the entertainment biz, son"—he was just a living example of why it was worth taking a shot going after the stuff of dreams rather than simply getting a job. I saw how much my dad hated working and realized he was right: Working blows. If you hate what you do, it'll always be work.

But what if you inverted that equation? Dad didn't have that luxury; he had mouths to feed and bills to pay. But after two decades of seeing how much he hated his job, I realized if you love what you do, it'll never be work.

So I fell in love with movies.

It wasn't hard. Dad would take me to see a new movie practically every Wednesday, with matinee prices around $1.75 to $3.50 by the time he stopped paying. We didn't ever talk much on the way to the theater, and we'd already dispensed with our reviews by the time we got in the car after the flick was over, so there wasn't a lot of chatter on the way home, either. But that was our thing: going to the movies. I never thought to ask him if it was more for him or more for me—his fat kid who wasn't good at much of anything except playing with *Star Wars* figures and memorizing *Laverne and Shirley* episodes.

It wasn't just movies with Dad, either. My father fed me comedy albums he'd bring home from a car-trunk record dealer at that job he hated so much: Redd Foxx, Bill Cosby, and most important, George Carlin—the master thinker/ speaker/funny fuck. Carlin would not only help bridge the generational gap between me and my father, he'd become a television touchstone for us as well. One of my favorite childhood memories is watching *Carlin at Carnegie* with Dad the night it first aired on HBO, a thousand years ago.

Dad was always my TV buddy. When I was a youngster, he'd lie on the floor on his back, head turned over his left shoulder to watch this giant twenty-inch console that looked more like a credenza than a television. I'd lean on his belly, propped up on my elbows, wondering if there wasn't an episode of *Batman* on instead of *Bowling for Dollars*. (If you wanna take a "Why didn't you just suck your dad's dick while you were at it, you loved him so much . . ." shot, feel free; I've heard how hard it can be for the limited to appreciate sentimentality.)

I was afforded one last opportunity to lay my head on Dad's stomach the day he died. Seeing my father motionless on a Philadelphia hospital gurney had me bawling, but I remember feeling two other things in that moment besides grief: 1) a distinct lack of life in what'd once been a pip of a guy, and 2) regret, knowing Dad was gone for good, and here this was the first time since my childhood that I'd had my head on his stomach and the last time I'd be able to do it forever.

We never like to think about the last time of anything, let alone the Last Time last time. But since I continue to be a reaction to Don Smith's life, I feel duty-bound to remember the specifics of Don Smith's death. The facts are these:

May 31, 2003: The Smith nuclear family and their spouses went out to dinner, following my Q & A at the Wizard World comic book convention in Philadelphia. It was a glorious evening, everyone talking, laughing, eating heartily, and enjoying being together. My sister and her husband lived in Japan at the time, my brother and his husband lived in Florida, and Jen and I were out in California, so it was rare that my mom could get all her kids together in one place. But man, could you tell they enjoyed reassembling the Justice League whenever they could. Parents *love* to view the fruits of their labor, and my old man was no exception. He polished off a filet mignon, three Manhattans, and a big slab of cheesecake while the rest of us jawed, and the more we talked, the more he laughed.

I loved making Dad laugh. He'd get really quiet, his whole body would shake, his face would light up as his eyes glassed over, but he didn't make a sound. Essentially, Dad laughed the way I cum—which may be weird for Jen or my mom to read, but it's true. When dinner was over, I packed Mom and Dad into a cab and kissed them both g'night, planting one right on the old man's forehead, telling him I'd see him in the morning.

That night, my father died screaming.

My brother and my parents were sharing a suite at a Philadelphia hotel when it happened. According to Brother Don, Dad woke my mother tearing off the sheets, screaming he was on fire. It was massive heart failure, and within minutes he was gone.

"What do you mean *screaming*?" I asked Don after he related the details of Dad's final minutes.

"He didn't go quietly," my brother observed.

And I hated that. Don Smith deserved a quiet, pain-free demise, because my old man did *not* have an easy life. He was born with a harelip and a cleft palate in an age when there wasn't much they could do for you. He'd undergone experimental cosmetic surgeries as a child to give him a more normal appearance, with his case even appearing in a medical textbook my mother once showed me. In his tweens, he lost a summer to further corrective surgeries. A childhood spent in bandages made him a painfully shy grown-up, though not too shy; he did pack enough charm to land my mother (who was by no means easy prey or a shrinking violet). He raised three kids on a meager post office salary doing a job he abjectly detested. He took shit from his parents right up 'til *their* ends. The least the universe could've done for this guy was put him to bed quietly.

But instead, my father died screaming. Tough shit.

That's when I started waking up. The beginning of a better Kevin Smith came with the painful death of his quiet hero—because that's when I realized that this life is a rigged game that you cannot win. Even good men die screaming.

Now, here's the important part of all this talk about cum and my dad, and here's what you need to remember in order to achieve and accomplish your dreams in this life. Please pay attention very carefully, because this is the truest thing a stranger will ever say to you:

In the face of such hopelessness as our eventual, unavoidable death, there is little sense in not at least *trying* to accomplish all of your wildest dreams in life.

Lemme include a strong exception: If your wildest dreams are to hunt humans or kill children, I'm not talking to you. Please draw no hidden, sociopathic meaning from my words. Life is fragile and painful enough, so don't hurt people, asshole.

Life is also, as George Carlin taught us, a zero-sum

game. We all lose in the end. We all die screaming. If that's the case, we might as well make for ourselves a paradise in this world. Make yourself happy and comfortable as often as you can, because sooner or later, the infinite hands you a bill for all these goods and services.

What follows is some tough shit. Tough shit to read, tough shit to accept. Granted, I didn't live through a mass genocide, nor am I a survivor of childhood abuse, so the title of this book may feel like an overstatement. If you want to read about real heroes and true survivors of horrible abuse, pick up *Shit Only Really Strong People Can Survive.* I assure you, I won't be the author of that tome. I'm the *other* guy, the guy who talks about cum a lot.

And the cum's gonna fly up in here. I talk about real life in these pages, and real life comes from cum. It's the only natural resource we don't fight wars over, as well as the one we're always the most generous in sharing.

It's advice; don't fight it. Either make something of the advice or simply discard it, but don't try to fight it. It's coming from the laziest fat fuck I've ever met, who came from a government-cheese-eating, lower-lower-*lower*-middle-class home and still somehow bent the universe to complement *his* will.

So this is the level of discourse you're committing to, gentle reader. If you have little stomach for this kind of cum-versation, you may not be able to swallow what I'm about to shoot at you. If you're a spitter, close this book, because from here on in we talk about some tough shit.

CHAPTER TWO

Pig Newtons and How All This Shit Happened

I t's very easy to find movie nerds on the Internet now—folks you can banter back and forth with about our nation's real national pastime. But back in the late '80s and early '90s, before the dawn of dial-up, if you weren't attending a comic convention in a big city, you had to stumble across fellow geeks in real life. And back then, geekdom of any kind, even for movies, was not as commonplace as it is now. Contrary to what Huey Lewis and the News told us, it was most certainly not hip to be square. When you wanted to find like-minded cineasts in the suburbs, it was more akin to cruising public restrooms: lots of sidelong glances at the urinals and foot-tapping under the stalls, hoping someone would get what you were after.

The first true film geek I ever met was Vincent Pereira, and ironically, we'd meet on what would eventually become a movie set: the same Quick Stop convenience store in

Leonardo, New Jersey, where we'd one day shoot *Clerks*. Vinny was a local high school kid the Quick Stop owners paid to stock the milk and mop the floors at night, but he was also *waaaaay* into film—so much so that he planned on *being* a filmmaker one day.

But I wouldn't know any of this for the first few months we'd work together because the guy rarely spoke. That changed the night he came in to stock the milk and found me watching an episode of *Twin Peaks* I'd taped from ABC the night before.

Normally, when Vincent came in at nine, he'd head right to the cooler, saying very little. That night, he paused briefly near the counter, recognizing the show and smiling slightly. He disappeared into the cooler as usual, but then reemerged and joined me at the register.

"You like David Lynch?" he asked.

"Oh, yeah," I said. "*Blue Velvet* is one of my favorite films."

In those days, you couldn't reference *Blue Velvet* without launching into a bad impression of Dennis Hopper uttering his immortal line "*I'll fuck anything that mooooves!*" (indeed, I had the Jay character bellow it in *Clerks*). Vincent was polite about how terrible the impression was and immediately launched into a discussion of *Ronnie Rocket* and *One Saliva Bubble*—two unproduced Lynch flicks he'd read about in a laser disc zine (if you're too young to remember either of those media-conveyance devices, laser discs were precursors of DVDs, Blu-rays, and digital, and zines were homemade publications and the precursors to blogs).

Vincent spoke passionately about film—about wanting to be a director. Before meeting him, I'd never heard anyone say they wanted to make movies. Nowadays, you can throw a rock and hit a film school kid. But back then? If they were talking about it anywhere, it wasn't in the central Jersey burbs. For Vincent, it was *religion*. I thought *I* was way into movies, but Vinny was into *film* and would teach me the subtle distinctions between the two (Vincent was a film snob long before there was an Internet). He'd teach me about aspect ratios, which were a new concept to a full-screen VHS culture. I used to complain about the black bars at the top and bottom of the screen cutting off half the picture until Vinny explained cropping and scope to me. Every week, we'd pore over the lone copy of *The Village Voice* Quick Stop carried, marveling at the cool cinematic shit happening merely a bridge or tunnel away.

When you live in the suburbs, the idea of driving more than twenty minutes to a movie theater is ludicrous. In Monmouth County, I had three cinematic options: the Atlantic Highlands Twin Cinemas, the Movies at Middletown, and, later, the Hazlet Multiplex. Each theater showed a steady diet of studio-produced fare—the mainstream blockbusters. In the Middletown theater alone, I saw *Return of the Jedi*, *Back to the Future*, *Top Gun*, and *Batman*. Whenever Vincent and I would read the *Voice*, we'd see ads and showtimes for films that were *never* coming to our local theaters or video stores.

There was a flick called *The Dark Backward* that caught our attention. It sounded so different and indie, featuring a cast we could trust: Judd Nelson, Bill Paxton, Lara Flynn Boyle—all of whom were going to be at a midnight screening of the flick, along with director Adam Rifkin, in an NYC movie theater called the Angelika, the indie film shrine on

Houston and Mercer. For two movie lovers at the ass end of the motion picture universe, even the notion of hearing the director speak and seeing famous people wasn't enough to inspire action. Drive to *Manhattan*?! At *night,* when all the crime happens? To see a *movie*? We were like rabbits, the species that never travels beyond five miles from the spot it was born.

The Pig Newtons, however, changed all that.

In *The Dark Backward*, the characters nosh not on Fig Newtons, but instead pound Pig Newtons. And according to the bomb-burst graphic on the full-page ad for that midnight screening, the director and cast were going to distribute an actual prop from the movie to every ticket holder: a free pack of Pig Newtons!

You'll meet no end of skinny busybodies in your life who'll tell you that if you wanna improve yourself, you'll put down the snacks. Ironically, it was the mere *promise* of a processed nonfood that would change the vector of *my* eventual fate. In that way, this fat man's life was *shaped* by junk food. So was this fat man's *ass*. And his *gut*, too. Also: his child-bearing hips and thunder thighs.

It was Friday night as we both stared at that sirenlike ad, the promise of props and the allure of indie glamour in the temple of film rewiring our programming. We mused about going to the screening as if it were a shuttle to Mars: "*Imagine if...*"

By Saturday night, we'd talked ourselves into it. The store closed at ten thirty; we called for directions, looked at a map, and did something nobody we knew or had even heard about had ever done before: We drove fifty miles into the city to see a film.

To me, the Angelika Film Center is what Maple Leaf Gardens in Toronto or the Forum in Montreal were to Canadian hockey fans of old: a magical structure where the impossible happened every night. The indie-est of indie flicks, serious cinema, could be found at the Film Forum, but the Angelika was something new and wonderful: an indie film multiplex, boasting five screens featuring the most high-profile indie flicks of the moment. We boys from the burbs got over the sticker shock of a twenty-dollar parking charge the moment we ascended the steps, proudly purchased our *Dark Backward* tickets like we were getting away with something, and stepped inside the ground zero of a burgeoning indie resurgence, the likes of which hadn't been seen since John Cassavetes picked up a camera. They didn't have a snack bar in the lobby; they had a coffee bar in the café. For the first and only time in my life, I ate a scone at the cinema. I was so drunk with culture that night, I didn't even care that I don't like scones.

The theaters at the Angelika are subterranean, so periodically while you're watching a flick, you hear the subways rumble by beside you somewhere deep in the earth's guts. It only added to the atmosphere, reminding Vincent and me that we weren't in Kansas anymore. Shit, we weren't even in Oz. This was the Village. This was New York City. This was indie film.

And the trailers before the feature were indie as fuck. There was no familiar voice-over—no narration starting with *"In a world . . ."* Indie trailers were a series of images or dialogue pulls, critical quotes hailing the picture, and huge title cards. The lack of identifiable studios like Warner Bros. or Universal at the heads of the trailers made the movies seem more important somehow—like someone had figured out how to make a movie *without* the usual suspects and gatekeepers.

The first trailer was for Hal Hartley's *Trust.* It was weird and wonderful, and all the characters spoke like they were in a play, not a film. The second trailer was for Richard Linklater's *Slacker*—a flick that seemed to not be about anything or anybody in particular. An art film. I nudged Vincent and nodded at the screen to indicate my interest as the *Slacker* trailer came to a close. I didn't wanna speak out loud; after all, we were in a church of sorts.

The Dark Backward unspooled, and while I dug it, it would not be the film that made me want to be a filmmaker. For starters, it had famous people in it. I didn't know any famous people, so I didn't walk away feeling empowered. I did, however, walk away with Pig Newtons—which were actually just Fig Newtons with a prop sticker on them. But that powerful, faux-snack talisman had worked its magic: Vinny and I had busted our indie film cherries with *The Dark Backward.*

All week long, I had to explain to my friends and family *why* I'd gone to New York to see a movie, then argue it clearly *was* possible to visit the city at night and return un-mugged. When he came in to mop the floors and stock the shelves, Vinny and I would plot our next move. We couldn't go back to our local multiplexes just yet. Stay down on the farm once we'd seen the Angelika? *Impossible.* The minute you start getting blow jobs, handys seem kinda dopey. The minute you discover a vibrator, your tolerance for getting clumsily fingered disappears.

So on Friday, August 2, 1991—the evening of my twenty-first birthday—Vincent and I closed up Quick Stop, took the Garden State Parkway North to the New Jersey Turnpike North, got off at the Holland Tunnel exit, went up to Houston and hung a right, and parked the car. One Kevin Smith stepped out of the vehicle and headed into the Angelika Film Center, but two hours later, a very different Kevin Smith would emerge. It was like taking the blue pill in *The Matrix*.

Richard Linklater's *Slacker* was the movie that *would* change my life. This shaggy paean to those who follow the road not taken offered me a glimpse into a free-associative world of ideas instead of plot, people instead of characters, and Nowheresville, Texas, instead of the usual California or New York settings most movies elected to feature. That Nowheresville was actually Austin speaks volumes on how culturally bereft and state-capital ignorant I was at the time. That night, Richard Linklater and his film not only captured my imagination, they kick-started my ambition. The simplicity of the story and filmmaking, the unpolished cast, the nontraditional storytelling—it was like cumming with someone else for the first time: Suddenly, you never wanted to cum by yourself again; figuratively speaking, this movie was teaching me how to fuck.

By the time we hit the turnpike tollbooth on the Jersey side of the Holland Tunnel, I finally said it aloud. "I want to be a filmmaker." I'd say that for a few weeks until my sister, Virginia, gave me awesome advice.

"Then *be* a filmmaker."

"That's the idea," I said. "I want to be a filmmaker."

"You don't have to want to be a filmmaker, just *be* a filmmaker," Virginia said. "Every thought you have, think it as a filmmaker. You're already a filmmaker; you just haven't made a film yet."

It sounded artsy-fartsy as fuck, not to mention easier said than done, but it turned out to be million-dollar advice. A slacker hit the sheets that night, but the *Clerks* guy got out of bed the following morning, ready to do the impossible. Most of the supposedly challenging stuff in life usually isn't as difficult to pull off as some folks would have you think. Believing in yourself and becoming a filmmaker is easy; only pull-ups are hard.

There's a trick to being whatever you want to be in life. It starts with the simple belief that you are what or who you say you are. It starts, like all faiths, with a belief—a belief predicated more on whimsy than reality. And you've gotta believe for everybody else, too—until you can show them proof. If you're lucky, someone starts believing with you— first theoretically, then in practice. And two people believing are the start of a congregation. You build a congregation of believers and eventually set out to craft a cathedral. Sometimes it's just a church; sometimes it turns out to be a chapel. Folks who don't build churches will try to tell you how you're doing it wrong, even as your steeple breaks the clouds. Never listen.

But before all of that, you gotta start with the *idea*. And I don't mean the idea for the story/movie/novel/installation/song/podcast/whatever. You gotta start with the idea that *you can do this*—something that's not normally done by everybody else. Since it's not second nature to take leaps of faith, you have to motivate yourself. You've gotta embrace a reasonable amount of unreasonability, because what you're saying is, "I'm gonna try this thing that very few people attempt, let alone succeed in doing."

But nobody else can believe in you if *you* don't believe in what you're doing. I've willed almost all the stuff I've done into existence, and if I can do that, anybody can do that. So start your chatter: Talk about what you're *going to do*.

Plant the seeds early and take as much time as it requires to will your goals into existence. Don't wait for God or Zeus to move you around the chessboard. God is busy and Zeus is doing movies now, so take control of the game yourself. Expect moments of discouragement; just don't wallow in them. When shit gets tough (and it will), simply tell yourself, "If an ass-hat like fat Kev Smith can succeed, then what the fuck is stopping me from doing the same?"

The only guy I ever heard of who got an amazing life literally handed to him was Hal Jordan. Don't wait for a dying alien to give you a magic ring; just do it yourself, Slappy. We can't all be Superman, but we sure as shit can train hard, and with loads of practice, we can be Batman.

And who the fuck doesn't wanna be Batman? Batman has an impeccable moral compass, he's clever and mysterious, and when fucktards get sassy, he punches them in the face.

CHAPTER THREE

The Shit I Made

Science tells us our dreams never last more than a few minutes. No matter how involved the plot may feel, we screen *multiple* five-minute minimovies in our cranial cinema every night. It's gotta be the same for the American Dream as well. While it's always thought to be about working hard, owning a house, getting married, and having kids, I think even *that* dream is subject to the same laws of nocturnal whimsy: The American Dream changes *constantly* and varies from person to person.

My American Dream has always been simple, and it's one I encourage you to adopt as your own: Figure out what you love to do, then figure out how to get paid to do it. Film would become that for me—a passion I got paid to pursue—but the theory can be applied to almost anything: If you like dogs, monetize your canine interest with a dog-walking or washing business. If you like jerking off, sell your sperm or wank for porn.

'Slike folks who start movie Web sites: They just love movies. Not sure what their endgame's gonna be, but writing about movies and hosting trailers is a start, right? For some, the endgame will be to make a film. For others, just having people read what they have to say about a subject they love is good enough. Regardless, the smart ones will always find a way to earn off it. Because once you've got a taste for working for yourself, doing what you love doing? You'll work ten times harder than any bricklayer or paralegal, but you'll never feel it and never recognize it.

Controlling your own little universe is key. Before I made *Clerks*, I was in my early twenties, and the universe I lived in was run by my parents. Since I lived rent-free under their roof, I had to abide by their rules—which included mandatory trips to relatives' houses every weekend. I wanted to find a way to be able to say, "I'm not going" for which I wouldn't catch shit. Being a filmmaker seemed like an excellent excuse to not go to relatives' houses.

So I got into filmmaking, and one day, I was able to say to my parents, "I can't go to Aunt Virginia's this weekend; I'm making *Mallrats*." My parents couldn't give me shit for not going to visit relatives with them because I was balancing multimillion-dollar budgets for movies about boys giving stink palms. But more than that? They were just happy I had a job.

And how'd *that* happen? How'd a guy like me, with zero connections or talent, *get* a job in the movie business in the first place?

It started with a movie called *Clerks*, a day-in-the-life

comedy filled with rooftop hockey games and necrophilia. It's a look at love and longing amid the potato-chips-and-cigarettes-selling counterculture that's become a true piece of Jersey history—a cinematic Stone Pony, if you will. It started life as scribbles in a marble composition notebook under the way-too-obvious title *In-Convenience*—a title my cohort Vincent felt was too precious and on the nose. One night, Vincent razzed me about going even *more* literal, eventually handing me a list of tongue-in-cheek titles that screamed the *exact* content of the script. At the bottom of his list was *Rude Clerks.* It was meant as a goof, but when you lopped off the adjective, the simplicity of *Clerks* seemed the most appropriate title for such a simple, bare-bones, no-frills flick.

Clerks was a creaky, spit-and-glue screenplay that somehow held together thanks to the casting of the two leads. We found Brian O'Halloran during a small round of auditions at a local community theater. He rocked a monologue from *Wait Until Dark*—which was about as far as you could get from the character he'd become best known as, Dante Hicks, the schlubby, Charlie Brown–ish register jockey at a suburban New Jersey convenience store who yearns for a bigger life, yet somehow still gets pussy.

If Dante's who I was, Randal was who I most wanted to be. I'd written the role for myself—which is why Randal has all the best lines. The character was meant to be part John Winger from *Stripes* and part Bugs Bunny, but really, it was just a fictionalized version of my friend Bryan Johnson—which essentially meant that Bryan Johnson was the guy I most wanted to be: the free guy who didn't give a fuck about what anybody else thought. The genius, Thelonious Monk said, is the one who is most like himself—and Bryan Johnson was unlike anybody else.

But the closer we got to production, the more I came to grips with the fact that I wouldn't be able to pull off playing Randal. The sheer volume of dialogue that needed memorizing was beyond my capabilities, so one night I asked Jeff Anderson—an old friend from high school who'd never acted before—to read the script aloud with me. By the end of that read, it was clear *he* was Randal.

But the stew needed one more special ingredient to give it a little kick.

Jason Mewes was a force of nature in those days, unlike anything you'd ever seen in real life or on TV or in movies. He was so weird and next-gen, you just knew something special was going to happen if you could focus people's attention on him. "Someone should put you in a movie someday," I'd often muse to Mewes as we bummed around New Jersey. Someone eventually did: me. I also cast myself beside him, taking on the role of Silent Bob—Jay's nearly mute muscle. If I was gonna go into heavy debt for the rest of my life to make a film, I at least wanted to be in the fucking thing; that way, years later, if I ever got the urge to do something stupid like finance my own flick again, I could pop in *Clerks* and see what I looked like when I made the worst decision of my life.

We shot the flick over the course of twenty-one nights, with a few day shots peppered throughout. The final cost was $27,575 and the film was selected for the Sundance Film Festival competition category in 1994. There, Miramax Films purchased the flick for $227,000. When I left Quick Stop to attend the 'Dance, I had a job. When I returned after the festival, I had a career. A clerk went up that hill, and when he came down, he was suddenly a professional filmmaker. I named my production company View Askew Productions.

This led to *Mallrats*, my then-notorious 1995 sopho-more film. Pitched as "*Clerks* in a mall," '*Rats* was a look at love and longing amid the twentysomething comics-craving suburban slackers of the consumer culture. With its sex and superhero obsessions, it was about fifteen years too early for any audience to give a shit. We were asking for a budget of three million, but the brass at Universal Studios insisted no movie could cost less than six million. When we pointed out that we'd spent far less than that on our first flick, we were told, point-blank, "Well that's not a real movie, now, is it?" The flick went on to gross only $2.1 million and represented the first of my efforts that critics would roundly dismiss, shitting in its foul little mouth.

Before *Mallrats* came out and died at the box office, I was already working on *Chasing Amy*. Our "comeback" picture was really just a very expensive therapy session to help me get over my sexual insecurities: A guy falls in love with a lesbian but can't get over her *heterosexual* past. I wanted to make it for three million, but Miramax balked at my dream cast of Ben Affleck, Joey Lauren Adams, and Jason Lee. But in 1996, Affleck's most well-known role was in *Dazed and Confused*, as the asshole senior with the paddle. Joey was another *Dazed* vet but best known as the girl who took Bud Bundy's virginity on *Married...with Children*. Jason Lee was most well-known for *Mallrats*— but since nobody had really seen it, he was most well-known for being confused with the star of *Dragon: The Bruce Lee Story*—Jason *Scott* Lee.

I'd written *Amy* for my three friends to play the leads, but Miramax had one of those stunningly original ideas: *bigger* names. David Schwimmer, Jon Stewart, and Drew Barrymore were three actors with whom Miramax had struck overall deals in the mid-'90s. Coincidentally, they were also the three actors I was being asked to cast in *Amy*. During the fight for Ben, Joey, and Jason, I was told by our exec, "This is a business. It's not about making movies with your friends . . ." That was a notion I decided to spend the better part of my career trying to disprove, starting with *Amy*. Instead of three million, I asked Harvey Weinstein to let us make the movie for two hundred grand with *my* cast. If he liked it, the flick was his. If he didn't, we'd be allowed to take it out and sell it to another distributor. It was the first of many times I'd sacrifice a paycheck or budget to get the cast I wanted or to make the film the way I knew it needed to be made. The gamble easily paid off: Harvey loved *Amy* and released it under the Miramax banner, Joey Adams received a Golden Globe nomination, and Jason Lee and I won Independent Spirit Awards. Folks who shit on *'Rats* praised *Chasing Amy,* and based on the maturity of the material, everyone generally agreed I'd grown up—a ridiculous assumption I'd also spend the rest of my career trying to disprove.

My fourth flick, *Dogma*, was pretty ambitious for its budget, but miraculously (pun intended), we pulled it off for ten million bucks. The story of two fallen angels and the Catholic misfits out to stop them from destroying existence boasted an all-star cast: Ben Affleck, Matt Damon, Chris Rock, Salma Hayek, Jason Lee, Alan Rickman, and Linda Fiorentino. But what I saw as a tongue-in-cheek-yet-still-reverent expression of the faith I was raised in was seen as the work of the Antichrist by the same religious groups who powered Mel Gibson's *The Passion of the Christ* to historic box office numbers. We received countless pieces of hate mail, three of which were death threats. The flick screened at Cannes and the New York Film Festival, garnering enthusiastic and supportive reviews, but when Miramax's parent corporation, Disney, started fielding complaints from church groups, Disney ordered Harvey to dump it. Harvey and his brother Bob bought the movie back themselves, releasing it through Lionsgate. *Dogma* became our highest-grossing film to date, and two years after its release, Norman Lear's People for the American Way gave me the Defender of Democracy Award for making the flick.

Jason Mewes had stolen *Dogma* right out from under the likes of Affleck, Damon, Rock, and everyone else, so it was clear he deserved his own movie. Following the Sturm und Drang of all those screaming charlatans pissed about my fourth flick, I wanted to make a fifth flick that wouldn't offend anybody except those with intelligence and taste. *Jay and Silent Bob Strike Back* was a valentine to the fans who put Rosencrantz and Guildenstern at the front and center of their own road movie. It was a fun shoot but a hellish preproduction, since Jason Mewes was still fighting his drug monkey—which in print sounds exciting, with the strong potential for bloodshed as man and simian fight for dominance of the planet!

In reality, Jay's drug monkey wasn't a *Planet of the Apes* refugee at all; it was a heroin and OxyContin addiction, which would plague him on and off from *Chasing Amy* forward. Multiple times over the next decade-plus, Mewes would spin through the revolving door of the finest rehabilitation centers California and New Jersey have to offer, fighting a genetic predisposition to addiction thanks to a mother who shot up while she was pregnant with him.

But even though Jay had his temperance problems like everyone else (mine was food, his was drugs), he was still a hysterically funny, crudely benign, true American cinematic original. Sure, there'd been buddy teams in movies since the invention of the medium: Laurel and Hardy, Abbott and Costello, Cheech and Chong, Bob and Doug, Bill and Ted. But thanks to Mewes's uncanny ability to say the most offensive or outrageous things and still retain audience affection, two stoners stationed in front of a New Jersey convenience store entered that pantheon as well.

Presented with the opportunity to tread the boards, Mewes took to it like masturbation. Acting was something he'd been unwittingly doing his whole life, enough to be naturally good at it. But while legions of actors in the business would sing the praises of Jay's raw, undeniable talent (indeed, Matt Damon was the first person to suggest Jay and Silent Bob get their own flick), other thesps with more traditional performance training on screen or stage resented Jason's outsider status. In an interview to support the second *Harold and Kumar* flick (not the first, mind you, the fucking *second*), Neil Patrick Harris took a wild, prejudiced stab at my boy.

"They were smart for actually hiring two actors that were actual actors playing parts, instead of hiring two sort of dudes that were those guys," the former Doogie Howser said in an Ain't It Cool News interview, overusing *actually* and its root. "They didn't hire like Jason Mewes and the other dude . . . Silent Bob . . . What is that movie *Jay and Silent Bob*, like what's Jay's name? He was this drugged out mess of a guy that was his friend and so he just cast him in the movie and filmed him doing crazy shit."

What an *asshole*. The guy who once played the genius child surgeon on television must've forgotten that was a *role* and apparently started believing he was hyper-smart for his years in real life, too. Shit, can you believe the arrogance in that comment, not to mention the hostility toward a fellow actor he's never met and apparently knows jack shit about? I called him out on it once, on Twitter, and to his credit the guy tweeted the following:

"Didn't realize the upset my words caused. Looked back at what you said and I concur. Ignorance on my part. Apologies."

Regardless, Neil Patrick Harris must've loved *Jersey Girl*: It was my first Mewes-less movie. It was also the second flick I'd have to bend over and take it for from the critics. Ben gave the best performance of his career, George Carlin got a bunch of screen time, and little newcomer Raquel Castro broke hearts—but nothing could save my first non-Askewniverse flick from the backlash beast that was Bennifer.

Thankfully, we followed *Jersey Girl* with *Clerks II*—my favorite of the bunch. Made for five million (a nearly five-million-dollar increase from the budget of *Clerks*), *Clerks II* was more than just a reunion flick or a trip back to the well, as I called it: It was the last good time. After that, film-making would change for me. After that, I'd realize my time as a cinematic storyteller was coming to a close. Because the tough shit is, sometimes you can start out doing what you love, and then doing what you love starts to become work.

Twenty years is a long time to do anything, let alone make movies. I've gone further than I ever dreamed. The plan back in 1991 had been to make *Clerks* on credit cards, hoping someone with money would see that we knew how to make a film and in turn reward us with a budget to do a next one. That was *it*. Imagine your plan was to walk down to the convenience store to get some chocolate milk, and while there, you were gifted with an entire milk production facility to run, complete with chocolatizer for all the milk. "*You want chocolate milk? You* got *chocolate milk, kid!*" And from that moment forward, for twenty years, chocolate milk became your life: the making of, sampling of, bottling of, vending of, marketing of, balance sheets of . . .

And while you love it all, this unexpected gift of a thriving chocolate milk concern, every once in a while, in the midst of it all, you think, "How'd I get *here*? All I wanted was some chocolate milk."

CHAPTER FOUR

Miramaxkateers and Shit

This is important to put right on front street: Nearly everything I've achieved in life since 1994 I owe to Harvey Weinstein—the larger-than-life (*not* a fat joke) half of the legendary Miramax siblings who mainstreamed indie film. And to show my gratitude, I made his ideals my own and fought his holy war against the studio infidels and heathens, sometimes even at his behest.

Now here's the tough shit: Miramax was owned by Disney at the time—the most studio-est of the studios. So in essence, I was an indie filmmaker owned by a mouse in short pants.

Miramax was the premier destination for indie filmmakers in the early '90s. Harvey and Bob Weinstein, concert promoters in Buffalo, dipped their toes into the movie biz and discovered art-house gold, distributing such envelope-pushing modern classics as *The Piano* and *The Crying*

Game. Their winning ways with non-popcorn fare caught the attention of the Walt Disney Company, and in 1993 the family-movie mavens purchased Miramax, lock, film stock, and barrel, keeping Harvey and Bob as coheads of the indie film distribution company they named after their parents, Miriam and Max. It wasn't charity on Disney's behalf: With a corporate wolf's war chest under his indie sheep's clothing, Harvey took underground film to mainstream multiplexes while producing a string of Oscar winners and pop-culture landmarks. Disney buying Miramax and the subsequent run of cinematic gems (and dreck) that would follow was the biggest boon to art patronage since the Medici family.

Harvey picked up *Clerks* at the '94 Sundance Film Festival, after its fourth screening and Q & A. The flick had built up amazing buzz over the course of its first three public exhibitions, and at its last fest run at the Egyptian Theater, Miramax acquisitions king and New Jersey native Mark Tusk would persuade Harvey to give our amateur film a room in their mansion. I'd go on to make the bulk of my flicks at Miramax, from '94 to 2007, benefiting from the gobs of Disney mouse money the Weinsteins had.

Under the stewardship of the big screen–loving siblings (who, according to their legend, got into the art-house game after mistaking *The 400 Blows* for an adult movie), smart and off-kilter flicks had a better shot at theatrical distribution— the dream of all nascent filmmakers. And Harvey could make your dream come true . . . if you were a true believer.

And the Miramax and Weinstein ethos was *easy* to believe in—because it *defined* independence. The brothers were modern-day folk heroes back then, mere years before they'd become figures of legend and myth, when their names would become bigger than the flicks they'd make. The pair had elbowed their way into the movie biz, bringing to the mainstream what was traditionally considered art-house medicine. They were scrappy and they had excellent taste, but it was their "Fuck you, we'll do it ourselves" attitude I always loved best—the fact that they'd achieved all they had as outsiders in what was normally an impenetrable field.

But worry not, gentle reader: I didn't drink the Kool-Aid. That's because, not content to merely imbibe the Miramax elixir, I *bathed* in it instead. I was in my early twenties, so I was espousing the tired old "Movies are for the masses; I only watch *films*" philosophy—the irritating, judgmental stage through which every budding cineast must pass. It was a point of view that synced up seamlessly with the Weinstein Miramax vibe—which was *Indie as Fuck*. In the '90s, Harvey sold the movie biz as an Us vs. Them religion—art vs. commerce. The best way to get young men to fight on your behalf? Give 'em a bogeyman and a cause. Our crusade? It was the Miramaxkateers vs. the Studios Suits! Never mind that our paychecks have a little drawing of Mickey Mouse on them, *THIS IS INDIE WAR!*

At Miramax, we were raised to believe that outside our fence was a world of waste: corporate conglomerates pumping out barely scripted sequels and remakes, starring the same old expensive faces the majors overspent casting yet again, backed by marketing campaigns that were nearly double the cost of the movie itself.

"They bought it" was a phrase Harvey'd often use when trying to explain a competing studio's better opening weekend at the box office. *Anybody* could throw money at costly TV spots to get the potential audience's attention; at Miramax we were encouraged to spend our wit and grit instead. We were making *film history*; the studios were making *product*. There was no art in their art; it was all dollars and sense-lessness.

Miramax was positioned as the antidote to all that, the cure for the common movie. And for a brief, shining time, it actually *was* the best game in town: *Pulp Fiction*, *Shakespeare in Love*, *Good Will Hunting*. All legendary, award-winning flicks, all of which had been put into turnaround by other studios. Harvey knew how to spin straw into gold from studio discards. The message was simple: The studio gold is shit and the studio shit is gold. The studio was where they spent thirty million dollars to make the same movies Miramax could make for ten. The studios were where they passed on a movie in which the Jesus Christ of Art-House Cinema, Quentin Motherfuckin' Tarantino, was involved— as Columbia Tristar had done with *Pulp Fiction*. In the Church of Miramax, Harvey was God, Quentin was the Son, and we were all full of the indie Spirit. Our films were just dirty little prayers.

But as with any religion, the moment it's organized, a beautiful idea becomes structured and institutionalized. Slowly, the gut instincts that'd paved the way for *Sex, Lies, and Videotape* and *Reservoir Dogs* were replaced with box office tracking and focus-group testing of everything from trailers to posters. The Miramax ethos went from "Beat 'em at their own game" to "*Two* can play at that game." Gone was the emphasis on creatively selling a flick or sending the filmmaker on a grassroots campaign to generate interest months before a theatrical opening; eventually, it was all junkets and reshoots for bloated flicks that didn't remotely reflect Miramax's roots at all.

Michael Eisner was the first person to notice it. We all met in New York City at the Disney offices to pitch the *Clerks* cartoon to Eisner and then-ABC-big-dog Bob Iger; Harvey was enjoying a number one opening for *She's All That*—a romancer that starred Freddie Prinze Jr. and Rachael Leigh Cook and looked and felt nothing like any previous Miramax release. As we waited for the elevator, Harvey boasted about being able to open one of *their* movies at number one, just as good as *them*.

For a rabid parishioner in the Church of Miramax, it was confusing to hear the Creator crow about topping from the bottom and stooping to conquer. *She's All That* was maybe a Dimension movie on its best day, which would've made sense: Dimension was the genre label, set up to release more mainstream flicks. The Miramax logo at the head of that flick felt somehow *wrong*. The emperor suddenly seemed naked, celebrating a Pyrrhic victory. I wanted to tell our good king that one more win like that over the studios and he might be coming back to Epirus alone.

But it was 1999 and I had no business objecting to how Harvey ran his company—particularly when none of my flicks had ever graced the top spot on any box office chart. I had a sinking feeling we were at the beginning of the end of something special and unique, but it was not my place to turd in Harvey's punch bowl . . .

Michael Eisner, on the other hand, unbuckled, dropped

trou, and crapped a long log of floating truth in the midst of the party.

Mere moments after Harvey's victory lap downstairs, we were upstairs at the ABC network offices in New York, readying to pitch the *Clerks* cartoon to Eisner and Iger, when my producer and friend Scott Mosier and I bore witness to how the heavens roar when titans clash. As we settled in, Harvey asked Eisner if he'd seen the *She's All That* grosses. Eisner congratulated him on the top spot, quickly adding, "But you've gotta be careful with your *brand*."

Eisner was the first businessman I had ever heard employ what would become the most overused marketing buzzword of the twenty-first century: *brand*.

As Mosier and I looked on spellbound, Michael Eisner was saying the shit I was thinking, observing that the Freddy Prinze Jr. pic would've been a more appropriate Dimension release. His theory that a Miramax film *meant* something to its audience—that the opening logo was a stamp of quality— was something even *I* knew. How could this suitiest of suits see this when our Fearless Leader couldn't?

"Touchstone Pictures used to mean something," Eisner said, referring to the Disney label that'd released the Tom Hanks hit *Splash* eons prior. "Then we put out a few bad movies under the Touchstone label and we lost the audience's trust."

Harvey looked like he got sucker-punched. He'd been feeling fine about his box office Benjamins 'til Eisner pulled Medusa's head out, freezing our per-screen Perseus in his tracks. That's when Eisner released the kraken . . .

"If you're not careful with your brand, you lose the audience."

The advice wasn't directed at me and I'm not sure Eisner even noticed or cared if I and my non-captain-of-industry cohort Mosier were in the room; still, I absorbed the cautionary tale like it *had* been intended for me. Never fuck with the brand. Check.

By 2005, after more than a decade of delivering Oscar gold to the parent company while still frequently battling with Disney over expensive, non-indie films such as Peter Jackson's Lord of the Rings trilogy and *Cold Mountain*, as well as such controversial films as Michael Moore's *Fahrenheit 9/11* and, yes, Kevin Smith's *Dogma*, the Weinstein brothers were done at Disney. They left behind what'd become Miramouse to start the Weinstein Company. It was like being Catholic during Henry VIII's Reformation: No matter what you used to believe, you followed your king as he made himself the supreme head of a new church. I followed along, as did Quentin Tarantino, the guy who put Miramax on the map. But without the deep Disney pockets, even *that* kind of credibility didn't necessarily get shit green-lit during the early rocky days of the Weinstein Company.

I remember when Quentin brought in a horror movie called *Hostel* that he'd shepherded but didn't direct. The cost was horror-movie small, with a budget of five million or less, yet the Weinstein brothers passed. *Twice*, actually— in script stage and after the finished flick was screened for them. And even though the budget was low, and even though their mightiest all-star was producing and presenting—the guy whose silver-tongued mobsters and glowing, mystery briefcase had provided Harvey and Bob with a license to print money—the House That Quentin Built passed on a minuscule-budgeted Tarantino project. Camelot was gone: Welcome to Came*little*.

Lionsgate seemed to understand the benefit of having a flick attached to a cinematic legend, so it picked up *Hostel*. It was a smart move, as Lionsgate did well with the leavings of the Weinstein brothers—just as the Weinstein brothers had done well with the leavings of other studios for so many years. When you're hungry, you'll pick through your neighbor's garbage, but when you're full you'd never *dream* of doing something so gross as touching someone else's discards. That's because when you're overfed and always full, with a seemingly unending supply of food, you tend to be a lot more wasteful. There's always more where this shit came from.

When *Hostel* opened well with a campaign that was straight-up early Miramax, it was clear the tables were turning: The studios (even up-and-comers like Lionsgate) had studied Bob and Harvey's marketing magic for years and simply started heading in that direction *themselves*. Imitation can be the highest form of flattery, but it can also be the death of your business if you do something specific that nobody else does. Once everyone starts doing it too, that's not good for business. If folks find out the secret ingredient is children's cough syrup, anyone can make a Flaming Moe. And the studios started mixing up Flaming Moes so tasty, the audience never noticed it *wasn't* Harvey and Bob behind the bar anymore. In 1999, I remember seeing a trailer for the DreamWorks release *American Beauty* and saying to Scott, "Wow—they're selling it like it's a Miramax flick."

And ironically, as the studios aped Harvey's Miramagic, Harvey started hatching posters and marketing campaigns that looked a *lot* like the generic studio sells he'd railed against back in the day. Look at the *Pulp Fiction* poster: Uma Thurman lying on that bed, the epitome of sexy and cool—a daring image in a thematically committed ad campaign. Now look at the Miramax posters from 2000 forward: The majority feature encircled famous faces positioned around or near a title treatment, with a tagline hinting at a plot. The marketing campaigns once so imbued with the Miramax attitude were being test-marketed to death until all that remained was a Denny's-like picture menu poster. Gwyneth Paltrow in *Moons Over My Hammy*.

There was no more Us vs. Them: We had simply *become* them. Like me, Harvey had started out wanting some chocolate milk, and he'd ended up being so concerned about running his milky empire that he sometimes seemed to forget what good chocolate milk even tasted like. Why use real cocoa and cane sugar when high fructose corn syrup is cheaper? After all: It's what our competitors are doing . . .

As the studios started making bolder choices, it felt like the visionary they were emulating was going in the opposite direction, opting to simply "buy" his openings, too. Sometimes the marketing costs were even double the budget of the film we were selling—as was the case with the five-million-dollar *Clerks II* and its ten-million-dollar marketing budget. Up was down, black was white, and the mission was muddled. It used to be all about *art* films at Miramax—art films that earned because they were simply better, or at least different. It had devolved into a desperate *business*, where art was rarely mentioned anymore and marketing spends crept higher and higher, with money blown on costly, competitive TV spots. I was now working for what was essentially the same kind of studio we once fought so hard against and were so proud to be different from. There *were* no more differences.

I'd become almost ecumenical in my thinking, waging a never-ending cinematic battle between art and commerce for my very artist's soul! I was an old man who thought in terms of indie vs. studio. But the tough shit? There was no indie. There was no studio. There was only Disney. And Universal. And Warner Bros. And Sony. And Paramount. And Fox. And one day, there'd just be a vast omnistudio — or a *network*, if you will — in which everyone in the audience would hold a share of stock and a small popcorn. All necessities provided. All anxieties tranquilized. All boredom amused.

There's a foreshadowing moment in *The Dark Knight* when Harvey Dent observes, "You either die a hero or you live long enough to see yourself become the villain." But perhaps the words of another fictional philosopher might apply a little better.

"We have met the enemy," as Pogo used to say. "And he is US!"

CHAPTER FIVE

Losing My Shit

I t started with Dante and Randal, the register dogs of
Clerks. It continued with T.S. and Brodie, the varmints
who infested *Mallrats*. It was the very foundation of *Chasing
Amy*. But I never had a name for it until *Dogma*, when Jay
referred to Silent Bob as his "hetero life-mate."

Over and over, my films focused on these intense male
friendships that basically functioned as same-sex, sex-free
marriages. These bromance flicks weren't like the raucous
R-rated comedies of my youth, where wisecracking anti-
heroes took on the establishment, pissing in the faces of
college or the military, boobs flying everywhere. The View
Askew films earned their R ratings for potty-mouthed frank
talk between dudes about sex with their girlfriends who
didn't understand their love for geeky shit, and how they
felt about *Star Wars*, and maybe even, from time to time,
each other. None of those flicks ever made more than thirty

million dollars at the box office, even with the brilliance of the Miramax marketing team behind them. So if you made 'em cheaply enough, you could enjoy a modicum of success—that modicum never surpassing thirty million.

Then Judd Apatow and the Universal marketing department shattered the bromance glass ceiling with *The 40-Year-Old Virgin*, *Knocked Up*, and *Superbad*, taking similarly themed R-rated comedies to hundred-million-dollar grosses. The type of flick I'd popularized was suddenly in vogue; when I saw this happening, I figured I was finally gonna get a piece of that pie. So I pitched *Zack and Miri Make a Porno* to Harvey over breakfast at the Peninsula Hotel, and he green-lighted it then and there on the title alone. Harvey dug the story of two platonic friends who're so hard up for cash that they make a skin flick to pay the rent. When I told him I wanted to cast one of the buddies from *The 40-Year-Old Virgin* to play the lead, Harvey was into it. When that kid's star-making turn in *Knocked Up* turned him into the now-bankable Seth Rogen, Harvey was ecstatic.

Made for thirty million dollars, *Zack and Miri Make a Porno* should've been an easy fifty-million-dollar layup for the company that once figured out how to sell a movie to the masses about a chick with a dick. Indeed, the internal scuttlebutt at the Weinstein Company, and even in the movie business in general, was that we'd do one hundred million at the box office—just like Seth's *Knocked Up* and *Superbad*.

"This is gonna be your breakout movie," people would say. "It's gonna make Apatow money!"

But aside from Judd himself, the Weinstein Company and I were missing a crucial ingredient in our home-brewed

Apatow stew: We didn't have Universal's marketing department.

Two weeks before theatrical release, the movie's moniker that he'd loved so much had become an albatross: Networks were refusing to play the *Zack and Miri Make a Porno* TV spots in primetime after one of the commercials ran during overtime of a televised game, prompting a father to call and complain that his school-aged son had been exposed to the term *porno* while watching family-oriented entertainment. How the kid would've noticed our spot sandwiched between all those family-friendly, liver-killing barley beverage and dick-stiffening pill commercials I'll never know, but it spooked Harvey into changing the TV spots. If you saw a commercial past nine P.M., it was for *Zack and Miri Make a Porno.* If you saw a spot before nine P.M., the movie was called simply *Zack and Miri.* One sounds like it should be banned in a few countries, the other sounds like you could take your grandma to see it. I'd argue that we didn't need primetime spots, anyway, because the hard-core subject matter meant the mallrats couldn't even buy tickets to something else and sneak into our flick. One night, while watching *Saturday Night Live,* the spot that ran wasn't even for *Zack and Miri Make a Porno.* It was straight-up *Zack and Miri.* Friends who marketed for competing studios would send me e-mails warning against the almost weekly changes in the selling approach. They said it was clear we were searching for a story, but if we didn't pick one, we couldn't educate the public about the concept. It's a bromance! It's a boy/girl love story that's a little naughty! It's an R-rated romp! It's doomed!

For the first time in my career since *Mallrats*, a flick I made received some billboards and bus-stop posters . . . all of which featured stick-figure characters against a white backdrop. We'd butted heads with the MPAA's ratings board over what an acceptable poster was, and, stymied at every turn, eventually wound up with the low-concept approach. It had an attitude but told no story. When you drove by the marketing materials, you didn't know what was being sold.

It was starting to feel like what had happened to *Grindhouse*. Quentin Tarantino and Robert Rodriguez made a double-feature exploitation flick complete with fake trailers and postproduced effects to make the prints appear aged. But what should've been an easy open netter shocked the film community when the Weinsteins dinged it off the pipe and sent it into the stands. But after seeing how much more they needed to educate the potential audience about *Grindhouse* when all was said and done, surely the same fate would not befall us. I mean, we had Seth Rogen for God's sake.

But despite the presence of Rogen, *Zack and Miri* did *not* get knocked up with a box office baby full of money. There would be no brass ring—not even a brass cock ring. The flick opened to just ten million on Halloween 2008. The scuttlebutt about *Zack and Miri* being my biggest earner turned out to be true, though: The flick earned a couple hundred thousand dollars more than *Dogma* to become my then-highest grosser.

But more than just the disappointment I felt in not reaching that magic hundred-million number that everyone insisted *Zack and Miri Make a Porno* could reach, that flick turned out to be the self-imposed beginning of the end for me as a filmmaker. I'd shot to relevance from obscurity making art-house films like *Clerks* and *Chasing Amy*—films that pushed at the edge of the envelope and said something new that had never before been cinematically expressed. But while it's a really sweet and charming dirty little flick full of funny shit that rests comfortably on the shoulders of Rogen and Elizabeth Banks (who knocked it out of the park), *Zack and Miri Make a Porno* is not me pushing at the edge of the envelope or imparting anything new; it's really just me running out of shit to say in movies. *Clerks, Mallrats, Chasing Amy, Dogma*—these were screenplays full of ideas that'd been fermenting for decades before seeing paper or celluloid, before a career in the movie business was ever even entertained. They were birthed in the daydreams and whimsies over a previous lifetime spent living at 21 Jackson Street back in Highlands, long before I ever imagined making movies myself. But as of 1994, I no longer *had* to dream about cinema: I simply *made* it, using all those dreams that were bursting at the seams.

But I haven't lived a life since then. I entered the dream factory in 1994, and by *Jay and Silent Bob Strike Back* in 2001, I was making movies about making movies. I was eating my own tail.

There's a lot of tail-eating going on in *Zack and Miri Make a Porno*, since it's really just the story of how we made *Clerks*, projected through a wet-dream prism, with Scott Mosier conveniently recast as a girl I fuck on camera in the back room of a McJob and fall in love with by the final reel. I tried to capitalize on someone else's success and forgot what got me invited to the party in the first place: the fact that my shit used to be *different*. Suddenly, I felt dirty, realizing I'd gone into career-management mode, just treading water, not saying anything new. I was making movies for the sake of making movies, saying funny shit, but nothing new. And when I realized that, I realized I was nearly done making movies for a living.

I was nearly done fighting someone else's war, too. At Miramax, we were trained to see it all as Us vs. Them. We were the rebels at Miramax, and the studios were the Evil Empire, filled with soulless Darth Vaders who lorded over the movie business on Star Destroyer–size soundstages and back lots. Art was carbon frozen and shipped off to rich Hutts to hang inert and lifeless on palace walls. And the whole time I was looking out at a galaxy of what I was sure were the bad guys, I never noticed I was standing on the bridge of the Disney Death Star.

But even as the phantom menace was slowly revealed and the Sith would hit the fan, I was still a loyal Padawan to my Jedi master, Obi-Weinstein. When Peter Biskind's book *Down and Dirty Pictures* painted him in an unflattering light, Harvey tasked me with writing a "Harvey's a good guy!" editorial for *Variety*. My pen a lightsaber, I ran through the infidels with my words.

Here's how good a cocksucker *I* can be when I really believe in the cause . . .

It feels like every year at this time, someone discovers that Harvey Weinstein is a tough businessman with a temper as large and legendary as his passion for cinema.

Whoa. Stop the presses. This also just in: The sun is bright.

With Sundance '04 well under way, this week marks 10 years since I was given a golden ticket into the film biz. The usher who brought me down the aisle and showed me to my seat was the supposed "Terror of Tribeca" himself, Harvey Weinstein. So right off the bat, you might consider everything I write with a grain of salt—as without Harvey, I'd still be jockeying a register in a New Jersey convenience store (which I'm sure, for some, is yet another reason to hate him).

But rather than jump on the recent bandwagon of unloading a character assassination sniper rifle into the Kevlar-tempered hide of perhaps the only truly interesting Suit (or, in this case, Suspenders) in the film biz, I'd like to defend a man I respect, love, and would take a bullet for: the last, great movie mogul.

As a guy whose first flick was dirt cheap and looked like it was shot through a glass of milk, I've been called a *sellout* by those who feel a move to 35mm ruined my artistic integrity (like I had any to begin with). *Sellout* is the cry of the garage band fan who wants to keep a good thing to himself; the kinda folks who'd govern your growth by insisting you never diversify.

But when Harvey (and by extension Miramax) is labeled a sellout for making *Cold Mountain* solely because the budget was almost 10 times that of *Pulp Fiction,* one has to wonder if the labeler forever quaffs from half-empty glasses. A sellout would have dumped that picture when their studio partner pulled out. A sell-out doesn't assume the entire, risky budget just so that one of the family can bring their vision to life. Had Harvey been the half to go south, leaving MGM alone atop the *Mountain,* would we ever have gotten to see how clean Nicole Kidman looked against the dirty south background of the Civil War? I think not.

Would a sell-out bother to release *The Magdalene Sisters* or produce *Dirty Pretty Things*? Because last time I checked, Vatican-denounced hot potatoes and organ-harvesting pictures were not boffo box-office bets. But it's easy to overlook the type of commitment to niche filmmaking it requires to put out a movie about Armenian genocide (*Ararat*) when you're ignoring the details and easy-gunning the misbegotten casualties of growing pains like *Duplex* (which even I haven't forgiven Harvey for). When it comes to the pursuit of cinematic excellence, some folks remain stationary, and others bring us *The Station Agent.*

Can Harvey be a brute? God, yes. I've seen tantrums firsthand that have been so outlandish, I was sure I was being *Punk'd* by Alan Funt. But in almost every case, Harvey was ultimately right. Turned up to 11, yes, but right nonetheless. This is the making of art (or, at the very least, movies) we're talking about; passions are bound to fly.

I'll take the shouter over the eerily soft-spoken, cold, bald studio exec who once invited me into his

office for a meeting simply to tell me I wasn't good
enough to make a movie at Warner Bros. (when I never
even asked to do so in the first place) any day of the
week. Given a choice between a clock-puncher with
his hand on the rip cord of a golden parachute and a
guy who, with his brother, set a tone every studio's
tried their hand at mimicking, I'm happy to wear a
spit guard on occasion.

And how weird is it when filmmakers and folks
who've worked for the 'Max come out of the wood-
work to eviscerate the hand that fed them? Most
of these cats never would've had the opportunities
they did unless Harvey gave it to them. You see any
other studio bigwigs following his example and offering former assistants the chance to exec produce
films? How many folks were beating down the door
to distribute *Citizen Ruth*? Jeez, what ever happened
to gratitude? Ah, what am I talking about? It's the
movie biz, Jake.

Bottom line, you can love a meal, and hate the
chef—but only hate the chef if he spits in *your* food.
Based on the quality of the quantity he distributes
annually, Harvey can never be accused of doing that
(unless you count that *Pinocchio*). Most critics of
Harvey would step on their mothers' necks to be as
successful as he's been at creating something from
nothing—to build, rather than inherit; to innovate,
rather than follow.

So he blows his top inappropriately from time to
time (alright, several times a day). Big deal. He's the
only non-actor personality in this business I know

who people will still be telling stories about genera-
tions from now, marveling at his repertoire.

In the dysfunctional family that is the movie biz,
I couldn't ask for a better father.

And while I can't put words in the man's mouth,
I suspect Harvey would sum up everything I've
written above thusly . . .

"*Jersey Girl*. In theaters everywhere, March 19."

Ironic, I know. The writer of that piece was a defender
of the faith. Now? He's more like Martin Luther.

I remember my friend Jon Gordon asking, "Dude—
'balding clock-puncher'?"

"That's Jeff Robinov," I confirmed. "He's that guy at
Warner Brothers."

"I *know*," Jon replied. "Everybody who reads that piece
is gonna know, too. You might as well have written, 'whose
name rhymes with Eff Obinov.' You sure you wanna burn a
bridge that big?"

I rocked him with a condescending cock eye and scoffed,
"Like I'm ever gonna wanna work at Warner Brothers,
sir . . ."

Warner Bros., you see, was the home of bloated, giant
event pictures with costly budgets—like the one Harvey
wanted to make called *The Green Hornet*. One day he asked
me if I wanted to write and direct what was going to be their
first big attempt at a franchise. When I asked him why he
chose the least obvious candidate for the job, Harvey asked,
"You like comics, don't you?" I signed on to write and
direct what was meant to be a seventy-five-million-dollar
franchise-starter for Miramax, but quickly lost interest

when all the meetings were about product placement and merchandising. The day they showed me designs for the Black Beauty before I even wrote a single word of the screenplay, I wanted out. This wasn't ever going to be *my* film: It was too expensive and it wasn't even my idea. So I wrote a script and ditched the sting of the *Hornet* directing reins, opting instead to make *Clerks II.* Lots of folks wanted bigger and better, but my heart was in making flicks nobody else wanted to make—which was fast becoming a dying business. And while Miramax was a haven for that kind of filmmaking, Harvey seemed to have a different agenda at the Weinstein Company—one befitting a start-up media company: Make only sure things. It was the opposite of what he'd taught his filmmakers: There is no such thing as a sure thing in the movie biz, so make the interesting thing instead. You can't count on the weather or the audience: Both are capricious and mercurial.

But many insisted they had the formula. The marketing team on *Zack and Miri Make a Porno* was throwing focus-group numbers at me for trailers and TV spots that flat-out sucked. "This trailer tested through the roof!" I was told by people who made the place sound less and less like an indie film studio. "Harvey listens to the numbers, and the numbers on this trailer are strong."

Zack and Miri Make a Porno opened on Halloween—Harvey's handpicked date, pulling in a weak ten million its opening weekend. After that, I buried myself in my library office and started fearing it was all over. Choosing to leave film is one thing; this was like having no other option *but* to leave film, because I'd just made a movie with the *Knocked Up* kid and nobody knew it was happening. You start wondering about your relevance. Am I a filmmaker people take seriously, or just the one-hit wonder Comic-Con clown?

Turns out I'm *both*. While promoting *Zack and Miri Make a Porno* at the San Diego Comic-Con, I was onstage in hall H—the massive six-thousand-seater where most of the bigger panels take place. The *Entertainment Weekly* sponsored panel was called "The Visionaries: Directors." Marc Bernardin from *EW* had invited me to sit on the dais with Judd Apatow, Zack Snyder, and Frank Miller—three dudes who'd all known the sweet taste of a blockbuster. One of these things was *not* like the other.

I may not be much at fucking you cinematically, but I can melt your mind with my oral skills. That day was no exception: I crushed on that panel. I'd been a Comic-Con fixture for years by then, and the folks in hall H let me know it that day with the warmest welcome and biggest applause. They knew I wasn't a Comic-Con carpetbagger who only drove down to San Diego whenever he had wares to whore; I'd been attending Comic-Con for a decade, obviously more fan than pro. That crowd reception and the panel that followed was the last good moment before *Zack and Miri Make a Porno* would open softly three months later.

Because Zack Snyder was on the panel and because the earliest *Watchmen* footage was being shown, the Warner Bros. top brass were in attendance. A half hour after the panel, my agent called me to say, "Jeff Robinov wants to sit down with you at Warner Brothers next week."

Yes—*that* Jeff Robinov. The balding clock-puncher.

I'd first met Jeff in 1996, when he was transitioning to Warner Bros. studio exec from being the Wachowski brothers' agent. I was working on the script for *Superman Lives*, and we didn't get along at all. Years later, we had an agent-engineered general meeting, which was fairly disastrous— leading to the crack in that pro-Harvey *Variety* piece I wrote. When I heard he wanted to meet after Comic-Con, my inner Admiral Ackbar shouted, "It's a trap!" Regardless, I took a meeting at Warner Bros. for the first time in nearly a decade.

The Jeff Robinov I'd met years prior and the Jeff Robinov I encountered at the meeting that day seemed very different, but the tough shit is this: *I* was the one who was likely different. I was more mature about my art. I'd done some cool shit and established my place at the table, and the Miramaxkateer in me had outgrown his ears with the name embroidered on the back. Maybe I was just ready to *hear* what a studio suit had to say finally, after being told for so many years that they spit lies and wallow in creative cowardice, and drink baby's blood.

When I cleared the propaganda out of my ears, this is what I heard Jeff Robinov say to me as I entered his office that day: "People here have been asking what I plan to do when I don't have this job anymore, and I tell them I want to produce Kevin Smith's talk show."

I was expecting an ambush, but it turned out Jeff just thought I was funny at the Con panel, and felt it was worth exploring whether my sensibility could work at Warner Bros. I offered to show him *Zack and Miri Make a Porno*, which he watched a week later. Afterward, out of what I assumed was studio politeness, he said he'd figure out something for us to do together. I didn't believe him, but I still thought he was a class act. He made the trip to my house to see the flick: You don't get curb service from most studio heads.

Zack and Miri Make a Porno opened (or rather, *didn't* open), and I figured that I'd never hear from Warner Bros. again. Indeed, on the opening weekend, I didn't even hear from Harvey.

I did, however, get a call from Jeff Robinov.

Jeff dug the flick and was seemingly invested in its success. He'd call or e-mail me with financial breakdowns and encouraging statistical data. We'd taken in merely $2.2 million on Friday night, but Jeff called on Saturday to say all the numbers were coming in double from the night before—which meant we might be able to crawl to a double-digit opening number (ten million) as opposed to the six or seven million the Friday-night numbers pointed to. He'd break down metrics like the flick was a WB movie. He kept me off the ledge that weekend and the next. This loathsome creature of the Satanic studios was my rock in a very troubling time. And I didn't even work for him or Warner Bros.

I was drowning at this point, holding on to a buoy for dear life; and instead of stepping on my fingers so I'd slip into the sea, Jeff Robinov—the guy I dismissed as a balding studio clock-puncher—extended a suited hand, pulled me up on deck, and gave me a blanket and cocoa. That's not the work of a faceless corporate money-machine; that's the kind gesture of a bona fide human being. I was a little sorry I'd called him balding, even if it was true.

About a month after seeing *Zack and Miri Make a Porno,* Jeff sent me a script for a flick called *A Couple of*

Dicks. It was a buddy-cop picture that I instantly warmed to because it reminded me of the flicks my father would pull me out of school to go see at a Wednesday matinee: *Lethal Weapon, Beverly Hills Cop, Running Scared.* A Couple of *Dicks* reminded me of the seminal action comedies I grew up watching.

"This script's hysterical," I told Jeff after reading it. "I don't know if I can rewrite it because it's plenty funny."

"I don't want you to rewrite it," Jeff hinted.

"You want me to be in it? Totally! Can I play Dave?"

"I don't want you to be in it either."

I was puzzled. I asked, "You want me to run craft service?"

"I think you should direct it," Jeff said. He felt that *Zack and Miri* proved I knew what I was doing with a camera and actors, and he wanted me to bring that sensibility to *A Couple of Dicks.*

At that point, the attached cast was Will Ferrell and Marky Mark. Negotiations weren't going well, as the studio wanted to make a PG-13 movie for the seventy-million-dollar budget, and everyone else wanted to make it R. Eventually, they all agreed to disagree, and Will and Mark went across town to set up the very expensive *The Other Guys*—a movie that did not resemble *A Couple of Dicks* in the least.

I assumed it was all going away. However, Jeff Robinov called and said, "You still wanna do this flick?

After the loss of their cast, I was shocked the studio was still interested in making the flick at all, let alone with me. Robinov said we could make it as an R, but the budget had to come down. It went from seventy million dollars to thirty-five million overnight. I opted to stick around to see where it all went, bolstered by Jeff's confidence in me.

And as if he didn't already seem like Santa, Jeff sure went North Pole with his next gift: They were going after Bruce Willis for this flick he wanted me to direct!

You gotta understand what that meant to me. I *loved* Bruce Willis. *Moonlighting* was one of my all-time favorite TV programs because Bruce's character David Addison was a living, breathing representation of Bugs Bunny on TV. Bill Murray was giving us *his* pitch-perfect, smartest-underachiever-in-the-room, proto-slacker in cinema (John Winger in *Stripes*, Dr. Peter Venkman in *Ghostbusters*) and here was a guy doing what we called "the Kmart Bill Murray" on TV once a week, in a sharply written, hilarious detective show.

Bruce Willis made fame seem *fun.* Once he got his foot in the door, he pursued passions that appealed to him beyond acting, like singing. I learned to drive listening to his album *The Return of Bruno* over and over, simply because the tape was jammed in my friend's car stereo. But it didn't matter, because we loved that album and the man who made it, the pride of Penns Grove, New Jersey, Walter Bruce Willis—the guy most of us wanted to be when we grew up.

I'd even been lucky enough to act beside Bruce in his most iconic role, John McClane, in the fourth *Die Hard* flick, *Live Free or Die Hard.* Casting director Deb Aquila had put me in *Catch and Release* as the chubby buddy of Jen Garner's dead fiancé a year before, and when she called me about auditioning for director Len Wiseman for a small but pivotal role as the Warlock in the new *Die Hard*, I said only, "Please tell me I'd get to be in a scene with the man himself . . ."

It was months later when I arrived at the corner of the Universal lot that was the home to the Warlock's basement. Len and his crew had been shooting the picture on the East Coast, and they were finally back in town to wrap up lots of stage shooting. When I got to the set, the bright-eyed and eager Len Wiseman I'd met months prior—the guy who loved *Die Hard* and couldn't wait to bring McClane back to the big screen—was gone. Len had a thousand-yard stare, the kind only Vietnam vets are normally known for. He'd been to war, it seemed—all that was missing was a necklace of human ears.

There was a marked difference the moment Bruce was on set. You could feel something change in the air. I assumed it was excitement—the electricity all must have been feeling simply because a movie legend was nearby. Shit, even when Len would *tell me* why he looked so grave and reveal the cause of his sudden peptic ulcer to be the star of his show, I thought, "This guy must be soft. If he can't handle Bruce Willis, it must be his fault somehow. 'Cause who's cooler than Bruce Willis?"

I was supposed to shoot on *Live Free or Die Hard* for a day. Instead, it stretched to four days. Bruce refused to shoot for the entire first day. Oddly, during the blocking rehearsal, he felt the need to explain to me *why* he was holding up production: The production had been filming for months, and every time there was a plot hole, they'd say, "We'll add that info to the Warlock scene." My scene had become a dumping ground for lots of exposition nobody wanted to deal with, so Willis felt the scene didn't make sense and needed work.

Eager to impress my new best friend, I said, "If you

gimme a laptop and an hour, I think I can get the dialogue where you want it."

Bruce liked this. I was sent back to Len's trailer to craft the scene Bruce was refusing to shoot. I gave Willis the pages, he gave notes, I redrafted, then he had the pages faxed to Fox.

But the studio wasn't happy with the changes—particularly a line about Boba Fett that had disappeared. They wouldn't allow us to shoot the new pages. That's when I watched what I then thought was the coolest move in Hollywood history: Bruce called someone at Fox, someone in a position of power—the head muckety-muck who wasn't Rupert Murdoch. There was a cell phone conversation during which I listened to John McClane essentially *be* John McClane over the new pages he wanted. I melted like a fifties teen girl seeing Fabian at a sock hop. Shit, I got as *wet* as a fifties teen girl seeing Fabian at a sock hop. In that phone call, Bruce was like a modern-day Harvey Weinstein, telling the studio—the very hand that feeds—to go fuck itself. Hard. I was in *love*.

But I was the only one. No matter who I talked to on that set about how cool Bruce was, I'd get weak smiles and strange looks. The person and persona I'd wax poetic about with his fellow cast and coworkers seemed to be regarded by most on the set who'd spent some time with him in the trenches as a fantasy.

"What a bad rap this guy gets," I thought. "They just don't understand him like I do. It takes a Jersey boy to know a Jersey boy . . ."

And this is what I was thinking when Jeff Robinov said

Bruce was their top choice to replace Marky Mark in *A Couple of Dicks.*

"I know: People say he's difficult," I said. "But we got along great on *Die Hard* four, and we're both Jersey boys, so I think he'll listen to me. This'll be fun."

Very somberly, Jeff said, "I really hope you're right."

CHAPTER SIX

Whatchoo Talkin' 'bout, Willis? And Other Shit It Took Me Twenty Years to Figure Out

I took an 84 percent pay cut from my writing/directing salary on *Zack and Miri Make a Porno* to direct a Bruce Willis vehicle that ended up being called *Cop Out*. Everyone on the cast and crew took less to work on the flick because we were all so excited to work on a Bruce Willis picture. Marc Platt, the producer, gave up his salary entirely to make the budget work. For a big, dopey studio buddy-cop flick, the budget sensibility with which the flick was made was Miramaxtastic. Bruce and I talked on the phone before shooting started, and he was warm, conspiratorial, slick. He said we were the Yankees. I insisted we were the Edmonton Oilers. We settled on the Flyers, because Bruce still remembered the name of NHL goalie legend Bernie Parent. We were gonna have a blast making a funny movie—his first flat-out comedy in years. I told him I wanted to make it as fun for him as *Moonlighting*.

A month later we were standing on set in front of the villain's house in Brooklyn—perhaps the friendliest neighborhood on the planet—when a glazier truck stopped at the light, affording the passenger a perfect view of a bona fide movie star in his backyard.

"Oh, Die Hard!" the dude yelled at Bruce, naming him after his most famous flick. "I got *Die Hard* one, two, three, and four at home, bro! DIE HARD!!!"

The light changed, and the truck pulled away. It was charming as fuck. Seeing one of the most famous movie stars on the planet getting love from his audience made me smile ear to ear. It was a plenty big smile, and it needed to be—as Bruce was frowning.

"You gotta love that," I said, desperate to make conversation with or reach this unhappy man. "So awesome that they still love you."

He asked if I wanted people yelling shit at me from cars all the time, twenty years after I made a movie. He glowered, watching the car disappear into Brooklyn as if the people in it were responsible for Holly Gennaro's kidnapping.

"People still call me Silent Bob and yell '*Clerks*,'" I countered.

He looked at me like I was a soggy ol' douche bag and moseyed elsewhere.

And that was Bruce for the *Couple of Dicks/Cop Out* shoot. The actor I'd worked beside in *Live Free or Die Hard* was now the actor who resented having me as a director. Like the characters he plays, Bruce doesn't do well with authority figures—and when you're the director, you're ostensibly in charge. So the moment I walked onto that set, he recast me from a colleague to a warden who was sentencing him to movie jail, where he'd have to wake up at hours he didn't want to and say jokes he didn't seem to understand.

On day one, we had a very simple scene to shoot: two guys at a diner, sitting across from each other, doing funny dialogue. This was in my wheelhouse: All I do in movies is two dudes talking to each other.

So when we hit the set, costar Tracy Morgan started doing the script as written, and Bruce started straying off the page. Encouraged by this, Tracy started ad-libbing. And when someone as gifted and crazy as Tracy starts bringing the funny, the guy who's *not* funny—the guy who is, in fact, the most dour person I've ever met—turtles the fuck up like Claude Lemieux getting a beat-down by Darren McCarty. I honestly believe that Bruce got scared that day; he's so image conscious, he appeared to worry that Tracy might outshine him. And rather than up his game, he went the other way: He shut down.

It didn't help that all of his cultural references were decades old, either. Tracy, like Seth Rogen, can give you eight different variations of the same scene, because both will ad-lib and write within the confines of the scene without altering it. They know each scene in a flick is there for a reason, so they play their game *within* the scene, polishing it, making the dialogue and characters more current and identifiable. But here it was 2008, and we were shooting a scene in which Bruce Willis starts pretending to see a bunch of people walking by in Brooklyn, off camera. Bruce's hip references?

Maury Povich. Connie Chung. Yoda.

After six hours of shooting, it became clear that once Bruce Willis became a *part* of pop culture, he stopped paying attention to pop culture. Every reference he'd make in the scene was from a time *before* Bruce was superfamous. He'd been in a bubble ever since—a bubble where Yoda was still a new concept.

I'd go over to him after each take and suggest alts or changes and try to be there for him, but he'd stare at me as if I'd farted, nod, and wryly confirm. Then he'd alter nothing.

At the end of day one, most of the production team met quietly to discuss what we'd spent the day doing: shooting half a scene with one guy who clearly couldn't wait to make this movie, and lots of takes of a guy who didn't seem to wanna be there at all. Even though Bruce waved off any direction or guidance, Tracy would spend lots of time between takes going over what was funny and what material could be explored further in the next take. Unlike Bruce, he'd flat-out *ask* for direction; he liked having someone looking out for him. The other guy? Well . . . maybe he was just having a bad day.

By the next morning, Bruce removed any mask of pleasantry altogether and showed me who he really was: the guy you had to get through in order to make the movie. But Warner Bros. insured their bet by surrounding me with the absolute best in the New York City film industry. Jeff Robinov tapped Mike Tadross and Ray Quinlan as my line producer and production manager. This pair of white-haired movie-biz veterans we called Zeus and Apollo had roughly three hundred years of moviemaking experience between them, having worked on almost every big show that ever came through the five boroughs. Whether it was emptying Manhattan for *I Am Legend* or shooting *Manhattan* with

Woody Allen, Tadross and Quinlan were there—the Rosencrantz and Guildenstern of the New York film community.

Mike and Ray surrounded me with an amazing crew that moved like the guts of a Swiss watch under their firm but friendly leadership. And lots of my crew had worked on the third *Die Hard* years back, so they weren't surprised how shitty Bruce was getting over a simple tow shot. While Tracy pretended to drive around Bay Ridge, Bruce was meant to monologue about a very important baseball card and its value to his father. We were shooting on what's called a process trailer: You place the picture car, as well as lights and cameras, on a flatbed truck and drive it. In the movie, it looks like a couple of guys in a car, driving and talking; in real life, the trailer rig looks more like a Macy's Thanksgiving Day Parade float, calling *lots* of attention to itself. Attention that it became clear Bruce didn't want.

As we parked on a block in Brooklyn to set the lights and get ready for our run, the locals would gather around the process trailer, curious about all that goes into shooting a movie. Add to that a movie star like Bruce and a TV star like Tracy, and you've got at least twenty people, pointing, taking pictures, or simply watching from across the street.

Willis called me over to bitch about how long it was taking to get on the road. The camera and rigging crew were scrambling all over the trailer making it safe, securing the equipment so it didn't fall onto the road and kill someone. Bruce started pointing out people and asking me what they were supposed to be doing and why they were doing it so slowly. He nodded to our cinematographer, Dave Klein, and bitched that all he did was turn on lights—which is kinda the job of a cinematographer. No lights? No camera, no action.

I tried to joke about it with him to lighten the mood, but he just looked at me silently, like I was telling him, "I see dead people." I hurried the already-rushing crew along, and within minutes we pulled out onto the city streets to shoot our scene on the process trailer.

We did a few runs around Bay Ridge before Bruce announced he was done. I hadn't gotten all the performance beats and information from the script that I felt we needed to complete the scene, but that didn't matter to Bruce because we'd shot what *he* felt was the most important aspect of the pages: his monologue. If I hadn't been such a starstruck pussy—like if it'd been Affleck doing this kinda shit?—I'd have shot coverage until I had what *I* needed to edit a scene together. And if it was a script he liked, a costar he understood, and a director he didn't loathe, maybe he would've been happy to oblige. But there was no happy for me whenever the Fifth Element was on set. The fun lovin' Hudson Hawk was actually just cranky ol' Bummer Buzzard—the guy who pulled me aside and strongly suggested, without a hint of irony, that I never call him to set before ten A.M. again. After that mini lecture, Bruce left—seemingly content he'd done well while the rest of us had somehow failed.

That was day two.

The rest of the shoot with him was just as fun. Bruce would openly bitch about how little money he was making on this show (he was the highest paid cat in the flick by millions, naturally) and dug his heels in to grind the production to a halt over the weirdest, dumbest shit. There was a scene in which the script called for Bruce's character to jump out of a parked car so he could race across the street to attend to his fallen partner, who'd just been fired upon by the bad guy with an Uzi. It's a panic moment, with the crowd scattering while candy-glass windows are shattering. We were doing Bruce's coverage, and when we yelled, "Action!" he stepped out of the car and *walked* across the street, looking more casually irritated than worried that his partner might be dead. AD Michael Pitt and I watched Bruce's low-impact saunter with mouths agape. At the end of that first take, I let Bruce know we were doing a second. He seemed genuinely shocked that I wanted to go again.

"I know you've been in a hundred movies where you jump out of the car carrying a gun, Boss," I said to him quietly. "But this is the first time I'm ever doing it. And I've been looking forward to rolling cameras on you running across the street with a gun, because it's so movie-badass. So can we do it one more time?"

Bruce rolled his eyes and waved me away. I went back behind the monitor waiting for take two, but Bruce wouldn't get in the car: He was just leaning on the driver's-side door. I went over and asked him if anything was wrong. He said he was ready to shoot.

"Awesome. I just need you in the car again," I told him.

"We already did that."

"Can you do it one more time on *this* take, too?" I asked in the same tone of voice I'd use to beg a chick for a hand job back in high school.

As serious as a Republican clergyman, he looked at me with disgust and said, "So you want me to get out of the car again, *too*?!"

The lazy, fat-ass settler in me felt his pain. The lazy, fat-ass settler in me, however, wasn't getting paid millions to make pretend he was a cop whose partner was being gunned down. So pretty please, with sugar on it—get in the fucking car and get out of the fucking car once more with feeling. The second (and last) take is in the finished film. If you'll notice, when we cut to Bruce he's already out of the car—that's because as tough as *Cop Out* might have been for some critics to swallow, it would've been a true spitter if they watched Bruce's character's ultrablasé reaction to a loved one whose life was in danger. It was so disappointingly close to the first take, the message was clear: This was the best he was going to give me.

Where was the happy-go-lucky charmer who made Maddie Hayes fall so madly in love? There were no staff limbo parties like there'd been at the Blue Moon Detective Agency whenever Bruce was around. The singing pitchman who made me believe that Seagram's Wine Coolers were a manly enough spirit to chug at a high school kegger? He turned out to be the unhappiest, most bitter, and *meanest* emo-bitch I've ever met at *any* job I've held down. And mind you, I've worked at Domino's Pizza. I signed up to work with John McClane but spent the whole flick directing Mikey, the talking baby, minus the Scientological serenity of Kirstie Alley and John Travolta.

"See if you still like this job after you do it for twenty-five years," Willis said to me once, on the subject of our chosen field of the arts.

"I've been doing it fifteen years, and I still love it," I countered.

I guess he took that as a challenge, though, since he fostered an unpleasant and unproductive working environment whenever he was on set. He'd bitch about not being shot first, and he'd bitch louder about not being shot *out* for the day, so he could go home. He hated night shoots and blamed cinematographer Dave Klein for not wanting to shoot the scenes in broad daylight.

When Bruce wasn't around, the shoot was fun and fruitful; when Bruce was on set, *A Couple of Dicks* felt more like that week I'd spent on *Live Free or Die Hard*, but with *me* in the director's chair instead of Len Wiseman. All that was missing was *my* necklace of human ears.

The days he didn't want to do dialogue were always interesting. Mark and Robb Cullen's script for *A Couple of Dicks* had been a Black List favorite around town—the Black List being an unofficial collection of the best unproduced screenplays in the business, as suggested by an informal survey across all studios. Originally, the movie had been set up at another company, with the screenwriters attached to direct Robin Williams as Jimmy and James Gandolfini as Paul. When that version was put into turnaround, Warner Bros. grabbed *Dicks* with the caveat that the Cullens step down as first-time directors.

This is all a way of saying that the script for *A Couple of Dicks* was well-liked, strong, and funny. So it was always a little astounding whenever Bruce opted out of doing his dialogue. Sure—an actor is bound to run into lines he wants to *change* in a script. But this was a case of a guy dropping his lines altogether—in the midst of *dialogue.* It's one thing to make a choice to play a *monologue* with a penetrating gaze or a single expression, but when you're one half of a two-person scene and you make a "choice" to not do *your* half of the dialogue? That leaves the other actor in exposition hell—because now the other actor has to deliver his lines and *yours* as well.

Bruce did this at the L&B pizza joint shoot in Brooklyn. We get to the set for a blocking rehearsal and Bruce tells me and the Cullens he's not doing any of the dialogue. His rationale was that his character Jimmy, who'd just been Tasered and robbed of a very expensive baseball card, would be so mad at Tracy Morgan's Paul for his partner's lack of intervention, that he'd simply refuse to speak to him in the next scene. As if it wasn't going to be awkward enough, he also insisted on wearing mirrored sunglasses so we wouldn't even see this groundbreaking, nonverbal performance in his eyes. Douche Bag Achievement: UNLOCKED!

So there's me, Robb Cullen, and Tracy, rebalancing all the *dialogue* into a *monologue*. Now Tracy has to convey twice the information in the scene, incorporating lines he never thought he'd have to learn. And as we got to the eighth and ninth takes, poor Tracy is struggling to even remember all the information he's suddenly had to impart in what was once a two-hander but is now more of a one-hander, with a guy who we're not even really sure is awake behind those mirrored glasses. At one point, he rocked us with his big move—he took off his sunglasses for a minute, cleaned the lenses with his shirt, then put the glasses back on. It was a little too David Caruso for my taste, and it didn't help Tracy one iota.

I'm a lazy, fat fuck, so I can spot my own kind pretty easily. At the blocking rehearsal, Bruce took one look at all the unsexy, expository dialogue he'd have to deliver in the scene, and I guess he suddenly decided two pages' worth of his half of the dialogue would be best not said at all—at least not by *him*. You can call that an actor making a choice; I call that an actor making a choice for another actor, and then making the double burden he's suddenly heaped on the guy no easier by barely being present in the scene with him. No fairness merit badge for the Last Boy Scout.

What made his "choice" even tougher to work around was the fact that he'd also dropped his dialogue in the previous scene. In the flick, Bruce is robbed of a valuable baseball card, and Kevin Pollak and Adam Brody, who play the nemesis cops opposite Bruce and Tracy, needle their cop frenemy about being the victim of a crime during their questioning. We'd shot Bruce's coverage first, as per his request, but rather than read his half of the dialogue with the actors in the scene, Bruce again insisted on doing it all with worldweary, withering looks at Pollak and Brody. This resulted in hundreds of feet of footage featuring Bruce not paying attention to the guys talking to him. It was clear the scene wasn't going to work with what he gave us, so Robb Cullen and I started coming up with new dialogue for Pollak and Brody to say that would cover the holes in the scene left by Bruce's "choice." At the *Cop Out* Film School, I'd slowly learned how to shoot a scene without my lead's complete involvement, so I knew we had the rest of the day to turn around and build the scene properly.

But suddenly, there was a wrinkle. Bruce decided to stay and do off-camera for the boys. This meant any rewriting to save the scene he'd fucked by opting to not do the dialogue was now not gonna happen, because when Bruce is on set, his will is law.

So we were shooting Pollak and Brody, and Bruce was

providing off-camera performance for his fellow actors—
which is to say he was sitting there, barely looking at them,
not doing the scripted dialogue. I had the boys looking at
the dead center of the bottom of the matte box to represent
the off-camera Bruce, and for some reason, this bugged Bruce.
He wanted them to look camera left or right instead—not at
the bottom of the matte box. It didn't matter that the director chose that eye line, nor did it matter that the director
was also the editor, nor did it matter that it wasn't even a
shot he was in: Bruce insisted we do one his way.

"Okay," I agreed. "Next take."

But Pollak and Brody *crushed* that take, rocking very
funny, pitch-perfect ad-libs I could cut into the scene, possibly saving it. I was happy and I had everything I needed
from them, so I indicated we were moving on with the
standard, "Check the gate."

"Whoa, whoa, whoa . . . ," I heard Bruce say to me.

I looked at him and asked, "We're not done yet?"

"One more," said the guy who wasn't even in the shot.

"Yeah?" I asked, kinda hoping he'd hear the lack of en-
thusiasm in my voice.

Bruce waved me over for a private conference, and as
I moved to do so, I said to the crew, "Flag on the play,
everybody. I've gotta talk to the director."

And you'd have thought I was Hans fucking Gruber
himself, the way Bruce Willis suddenly *turned* on me, saying,
"We got a problem here?"

I was wide-eyed. This man had such an issue with my
dopey director comment—a comment that was based on
fact, since the man was now literally calling the shots in this

scene—that he was stepping to me in front of the entire cast and crew.

"I don't have a problem," I said. "But it sounds like you do, Boss."

"Well maybe you should clear the set so we can talk about it," he said, giving me the hard McClane stare.

"You want me to clear the set?" I asked, trying to hide the terror I was feeling. From where Bruce was standing, he could easily hit me: He was in striking distance (movie nerd alert: He was also in *Striking Distance*). "Okay . . ." And to everyone in that tiny, fake baseball card store, I said, "Can you take five, folks? Outside."

When everyone was gone, he yelled at me for not taking his suggestion. I said I had everything I needed for the scene and that I *liked* the eye line that I'd *asked* Pollak and Brody to give me.

Then, out of nowhere, he asked if I wanted to hit him.

It was fucking insane. I'd compare it to high school theatrics, but I'd never engaged in so petty and faux-macho a standoff in my teens. And worse? We were wasting time and money—just so this lion in winter could show me he still had teeth. Me: the guy who took the 84 percent pay cut to make the movie with the big, stupid jerk.

I kept composed and said we'd bring everyone back and shoot it *his* way. Then I went outside and told everyone to come back in and get ready for one more take of the same setup. Following that, I walked half a block to my trailer, locked myself inside the bathroom, and put my fist through the wall three times.

It sounds more impressive than it is, as trailer walls are

pretty paper-thin. But it wasn't the actual damage that was so out of character for me; it was the throwing of a punch — even at an innocent wall. This man managed to get me in as emotionally confounding and confused a space as my wife could in the midst of our worst arguments. But I could fuck Jen and blow off steam; I didn't have that luxury with Bruce. The frustration Willis created that day turned me into Cuba Gooding Jr. in *Boyz n the Hood* — swinging at the air, trapped in the mouth of madness. And for the rest of the show, whenever someone used my trailer bathroom and emerged asking about the three giant holes decorating the walls, my assistant Meghan would say, "We've named those holes Die Hard One, Die Hard Two, and Die Hard Three."

I think it comes down to this: Bruce has been sitting behind directors for years, watching them make TV and film. You do that long enough, you know as much as everyone on set: You know how all the departments work, you've had experience shooting stuff that doesn't make the cut, and chances are you've been around more movies than anyone else in the cast or on the crew. At that point, many actors simply make the transition to directing — Robert Redford, Kevin Costner, and Ben Affleck leap to mind.

Bruce would be an amazing director, as he's accumulated a shit-ton of moviemaking ability, simply by being in as many flicks as he has over his whole career. But instead, Bruce simply opts for telling people what to do on *their* sets. Sadly, he only tells you what a shitty job you're doing, shaking his head like nobody understands cinema except *him*.

If you're going through hell, as the adage says, keep going — 'til you get out of hell altogether. One of the things that helps you focus less on an undesirable present is the eternal promise of a hopeful future. So while I was earning condescending looks from Walter Bruce simply for doing the job I was hired to do, I was dreaming of *Hit Somebody*— the hockey movie I intend to be my last film.

When I got to the *Dicks* set, I had my heart set on casting Bruce as a grizzled hockey vet who dies on the ice. In preparation for this, I bought a glass desktop hockey puck trophy case, which colorfully displayed all the pucks of every World Hockey Association team that ever hit the ice. It was meant to be bait.

The idea was simple: I always cut the flicks I shoot during production and invite cast and crew to visit the editing room anytime they want to see their work put together the way it'll look in the finished film. I've been doing this since *Jay and Silent Bob Strike Back*—and sharing it with the cast and crew, who always love seeing the flick take shape day by day. Always be a big includer, kids; exclude folks, and you're excluding their possibly good ideas as well.

So in my head, the scene would go like this: Bruce would eventually come to the editing room after my many invites. And while I'd screen his cut footage for him, he'd see that glass puck case sitting atop a speaker and ask, "What's this?" And then I'd hit him with three periods full of hockey talk and *Hit Somebody* highlights—during which he'd learn all about the character I was writing for him. And he'd say, "Gimme a script as soon as it's done." And eventually, Bruce Willis would play that role in my flick and win the Academy Award doing so, or other plaudits I always felt he deserved but never saw him receive. I'd show the world how cool and talented the Pride of Penns Grove really was. And

Bruce would love it because, finally, he wouldn't have a gun in his hand as he ran around on the screen; he'd be skating, brandishing a hockey stick instead.

That was before I put my fist through the nearly cardboard trailer walls. I returned to the editing room that night, took the glass hockey puck case off the speaker, and hid it in the back of the closet.

Thank God for weed, is all I can say. At the end of every workday, I'd go back to my apartment, spend time with my family, then blaze out and edit the previous day's raw footage. It didn't occur to me to bake a smoking lunch to bring to set until halfway through the show, when I saw Willis having a drink one afternoon. It was nothing scandalous: just a lunchtime stiff one. Dude's entitled—he's a grown adult. But so am I. So as grown adults were making choices to imbibe alcohol with their lunches, I'd smoke up in my trailer and play NHL 08 with friends and various puck-heads from the crew. I should've spent lunches napping, since I wouldn't get much sleep at nights, editing 'til the wee hours of the morning. But a nap wouldn't make working with Bruce easier to take—THC would. By the end of lunch, it was back to work on the set, crisp and ready to roll with oceans more tolerance for Mr. Morose.

To be fair, Bruce wasn't always doom and gloom on the *Cop Out* set. One time, I saw him lose it and laugh hysterically. We were between takes at video village—the arrangement of monitors that allows you to see exactly what the camera's seeing, so everyone on set has a general idea of what's being seen in the frame. My friend Malcolm was cracking people up when Bruce told us all we didn't know comedy. He asked us if we wanted to see true comedy. A laptop was brought over and Bruce instructed us to go to YouTube and look up Red Rose Tea. In doing so, we were presented with an old black-and-white commercial from the '60s. It was a spot for Red Rose Tea in which chimpanzees in suits were "playing" instruments and "singing" over and over, "Red Rose Tea. Red Rose Tea!" At first, it was charming to see Willis crack up at the clip: Apparently, all mirth hadn't abandoned him yet, and maybe Anakin Skywalker was still buried somewhere behind that mask. But upon the third straight viewing of the primate pitchmen, when the laughter was over for everyone but Bruce, I started to wonder if the apes were still alive and if they were available for day-play on the show—simply to put a goddamn smile on this man's face while he was on set. It seemed that the only way to the eight-hundred-pound gorilla's heart was with a bunch of chimps.

Following years of anti-Hollywood sentiment at Miramax, I believed the studio was the enemy. But in reality, the studio was lovely every step of the way. Even when they told us we were going to have to change the title *A Couple of Dicks*, they were more collaborative than condescending. Having seen what I'd gone through with the ratings board on *Zack and Miri Make a Porno*, Warner Bros. called the networks and asked if they'd have trouble running spots for a buddy-cop movie cheekily entitled *A Couple of Dicks*. The networks said they loved the title but wouldn't run the spots before nine at night. The studio explained that they couldn't be expected to market the movie effectively if they couldn't run TV spots before nine, so they asked for a title change. Producer Adam Siegel and I were deflated that we had to trash an entire sequel campaign hatched with Robb Cullen for *Dicks 2: Dicks Come Again*, with poster taglines like "Things just got harder" or "Get Dicks-slapped!"

The *Cop Out* budget was thirty-five million dollars, but since we shot fewer full days than all the half days on the other flicks I've ever shot *combined*, we brought the flick home for thirty-two million—saving money, just like we always tried to do at Miramax. All that propaganda I'd been fed about how the studios didn't care about their flicks and how all the execs were just collecting paychecks? Utter horseshit.

Not only had I spent my entire career stupidly believing in the anti-studio rabble, I was plagued by other childlike beliefs as well: I'd given up lots of money to work beside a guy I'd made a hero in my head. And not because he played a hero in the movies, but because he'd *made it*: Like me, Walter Bruce Willis was born at the asshole end of the showbiz universe, with no apparent means of entry and no Hollywood pedigree, and he *still* got through the gates. As David Addison, he gave me laughs, sure; but more important, he gave me *hope*—hope that maybe one day, *I* could be in the movie biz, too. But who we want or need people to be and who they really are tend to be miles apart—especially in the movies.

It was some tough shit because I genuinely liked the Bruce Willis *persona* and imagined Bruce Willis might be cool, too. But at the end of the day, he wasn't cool and he wasn't a miserable person: He was just a movie star. We project identities onto movie stars, forgetting most are really just blank canvases across which some very cool performances can happen. I projected a personality onto Bruce and was ill-prepared to deal with the reality. While I'd read about Hollywood for years, I'd never worked with a bona fide movie star before (please don't tell Ben Affleck I said that). Ultimately, the only thing that mattered, I guess, was if Bruce was good at *playing* a hero. And he was: always has been, always will be. The great pretender.

You know who the *real* hero on *Cop Out* was? Tracy Morgan. Severely diabetic, Tracy was going through a particularly tough foot episode during the shoot, requiring him to wear a medical boot fixed with a draining device between every take. The hole in Tracy's foot should've prohibited the guy from even working, let alone running around a movie set pretending to be a cop. Yet even with that, he gave 100 percent and beyond for the show. It was Tracy who kept the show going. Tracy—the guy who'd make everyone laugh while he was nursing a damaged foot you could see through. He, too, came to work with a legend and he, too, learned pretty fucking quickly that the guy he showed up to be in a movie beside didn't exist anymore—if he ever did at all.

It may not have played out in the finished film, but every day on the set of *Cop Out*, we'd watch a hero trapped in the wrong place at the wrong time try to do some good, running around with cut-up feet. But sadly, in *our* production of *Die Hard*, Tracy was John McClane, and John McClane became the flick's very own Hans Gruber.

To whom I say, *"Yippie ki-yay, moviefucker."*

CHAPTER SEVEN

Weed, Gretzky, and Getting My Shit Together

For years, I'd made movies about stoners—all while having smoked weed less than ten times total in my entire life. I'd known exactly one stoner ever—Jason Mewes— and he hardly qualified, as he barely went green before dancing with Mr. Brownstone. Mewes may have portrayed a stoner, but in reality he was just passing through Weedville on his way to harder, scarier shit. We were a couple of frauds (or actors), yes; but it'd be those fraudulent flicks I'd made that would eventually put me on a set with the man who would become my ganja guru and place me on the pathway to enlightenment, bliss, calm, and creativity.

Seth Rogen is a genius—there's just no two ways about it. He's a comedic genius who can write on his feet. He's a life genius, too, as far as I'm concerned, because the dude cracked the code for me. Seth was the most productive pot smoker I'd ever met, and he never seemed remotely fucked up. Here was a guy who could not only handle *his* high, he could handle your high, your friends' highs, *and* your mom's high—all while getting lots of shit done. I'd never known anyone like that before, and even though I'd always been pretty straight-edge, I found it appealing and somewhat enviable.

I loved watching Rogen's razor-sharp wit build joke after joke in the middle of the scene, while cameras rolled, with little prep, making every frame usable. But as much as he gave me on the *Zack and Miri Make a Porno* set, it was what he gave me *off* the set, after we wrapped, that'd change everything.

Right now, every bear and bear-loving twink is hoping the next paragraph is about me and Seth Rogen sharing his joint. If you wanna stop right here so you can tug one out— the image of two zaftig, bearded, fluffy funny boys bouncing into each other with their wieners in the splintered jerk-drawer of your mind's eye—read no further.

What really happened was that I smoked some weed with Seth.

When the flick wrapped, I asked the king of the stoners if he wanted to spark a celebratory joint in the editing room that night. We blazed and reviewed the entire shoot, laughing while watching outtakes, and freely conversed in a way I hadn't in years. Rogen talked about how influential *Clerks* was and I talked about my favorite part of *The 40-Year-Old Virgin*—when Seth is playing a fighting video game with Paul Rudd, winning, and narrating what's happening on screen—his character beheading Rudd's. I lost my shit and rewound five times, just to hear him say, "I'm ripping your head off; now I'm throwing it at your body.

FUCK YOU!" It was a fun night. It was candid and honest. It was weed. I loved it.

But I was Captain Responsibility, so I didn't smoke again for another three months. Even though I'd partaken of God's own air and found a better version of me waiting there after I exhaled, I still had misinformed notions of what weed did and was: I didn't think I could work *and* smoke.

So it wasn't 'til after I wrapped the edit on *Zack and Miri* that I indulged again—this time on Fourth of July 2007. Jen's parents had taken Harley out of town, up to Big Bear, leaving Jen and me the whole house to ourselves. And since I grew up part of a family of five, in a small, one-floor, three-bedroom house, whenever there's an empty house, my mind immediately turns to transgression. When I lived with my parents, as soon as they left the house for a few hours, I'd try to get *something* accomplished that was either frowned upon or flat-out against the rules. There wasn't much logic to it other than "Nobody's here to say no . . ."

That instinct has never gone away. Even though I live in a house with enough distance between me and my kid's rooms that she'll never even suspect her parents are fucking, let alone *hear* 'em, I still get rock-hard erections when nobody else is home but me and Jennifer. This is all heightened by the fact that my wife fucks in a style I can only describe as "high school fun-tastic": Even though I've been fucking this same woman for the past dozen years, she *still* induces in me the crazed hormonal hysteria I've only otherwise felt back in high school during those heady (and head-y) days of what my grandmother adorably dubbed "teenage titty-twistin' and freshman finger-bangin'." Every time I have sex with Jen Schwalbach, it feels like we're getting away with something. It's transgressive while being about as un-Hollywood as you can imagine (two people having monogamous sex, alone in a bed). Schwal-Doll pops with the sexy in such a way that even when my in-laws are around, I hotly pursue like Pepé Le Pew.

So with all of our loved ones away, we spun the wheel of naughty to figure out what we could do in our house that'd feel dirty and wrong enough while still being safe and post-coital sensible: Nobody wants to cum and *then* come to their senses. We remembered some weed that her friend had given us for Christmas years prior, which had sat in the safe forever, waiting to be smoked. Getting stoned while alone in the home we owned on the Fourth of July not only sounded sexy and naughty, I imagined it'd have the same disconnected, vaguely patriotic feeling I got whenever I watched *Saving Private Ryan*. So five years into our marriage, Schwalbach and I rolled really bad joints and set about getting stoned together in our empty house.

To say it was glorious, dear reader, is to short-sell an orgasm as feeling about as good as a stretching yawn: There's just no comparison. We smoked and had amazing conversations full of humor, love, and truth. We called a cab and ate tons of cotton candy at the Simon L.A. restaurant, making out under the stars on the outdoor couches like we were sophomores at the lunch table who'd spent last period apart.

Then we fucked. Lots. And it rocked. It was an inhibition-free, total surrender to married carnality. I even took my shirt off.

And I *liked* who I was when I was smoking weed. I liked Stoner Kev so much. He was relaxed. He couldn't care less about the movie biz or where he stood in it. He spent less energy trying to make people laugh because he was laughing lots *himself*. At that point in my life, weed was exactly what I needed.

So at age thirty-seven, I started smoking weed every day. I made a deal with myself: If I was going to smoke weed, I had to tie it to something creative. If I was blazing, I was writing, podcasting, or editing at the same time—same way I did with cigarettes. I wouldn't allow myself to simply smoke weed and watch movies or TV; if I was going to be irresponsible every day, I had to couple it with productivity. I decided to get my work done by five P.M., then indulge in an evening smoke while writing.

After a month, I wondered why I'd set that arbitrary five P.M. smoking start time. I didn't have a job-type job and I wasn't a vampire, so what the fuck was I waiting 'til sundown for? The start time moved up to one/two-ish o'clock, post-lunch.

The turning point was the opening weekend of *Zack and Miri Make a Porno*, starring the dude from *Knocked Up* and *Superbad*. Sadly, it was made by the guy who did *Jersey Girl* and marketed by the people who sold *Hoodwinked Too!* Seth Rogen's amazing streak of R-rated comedy success at the box office had been broken. By me.

That's the day I became a wake-and-baker.

I'd rise in the morning, head down to my office, and start blazing. I didn't go near the Internet for fear I'd be crucified or chased with pitchforks and torches after putting a stink on Seth. Instead, I started pulling sealed DVDs off my library shelves—movies that'd been purchased but never viewed, most still as wrapped in plastic as Laura Palmer. I'd always overbought at the DVD store because I assumed one day, I'd have enough time to watch all the flicks in my DVD library. I imagined, somehow, I'd end up paralyzed—and if that was the case, I was gonna be prepared to watch a shit-ton of movies. This is the only reason I can think of for why I would've possibly bought the copy of *Baby Mama* that stares down at me from my library shelf, unopened.

Turns out the paralysis I was preparing for was creative paralysis: I didn't want to make Kevin Smith movies anymore. Some critics would've been happy to hear that, as they didn't want to *see* any Kevin Smith movies anymore, but I couldn't share that information with the world. What would they possibly say if they knew I was losing interest in making bromances? I started making those flicks because they didn't exist, but now lots of folks were doing movies about dudes in platonic love with one another. There was a hole and it had been filled. But who would I be if I wasn't the *Clerks* guy? What would I do with myself if I wasn't making movies any longer? "How the fuck can you even *think* about walking away from a gig this sweet, you fat asshole?!?" I asked myself.

And into my weed-induced coma came a ray of light, carried by a DVD box set special-ordered from Canada. *Hockey: A People's History* had sat on my shelf forever, purchased like all the other sealed DVDs in my collection for some future version of myself who'd have the time to enjoy it. And there I was in my self-imposed exile from the Internet, between projects, with lots of time to kill.

I broke my own rule and started smoking weed and *not*

being creative. Instead, I'd blaze and passively *watch* TV—
or, rather, a DVD box set of a Canadian documentary series
that was the northern equivalent of Ken Burns's *Baseball*.
The more I smoked, the more the Canadiana seeped into my
pores. Emotional tale after tale told the epic of a self-made
land full of practical dreamers who loved and understood
the importance of something so seemingly silly as this kids'
game. Their struggles became *my* struggles. I went through
one disc after another like I was catching up on a season of
Weeds or *Lost*. I'd burst into my bedroom down the hall
periodically and download on my wife astounding hockey
facts and trivia—none of which she cared a tin whistle about
as she smiled at her husband who was suddenly passionate
about something other than pussy and movies.

Because what's *not* to connect with about the culture of
hockey?

1. In hockey, you get to watch sixty minutes of the
   most in-shape athletes on the planet rocket across
   the surface of a giant fucking diamond.
2. People literally walk on water in hockey. Granted,
   the water is frozen, but still: The last guy to popu-
   larize water-walking got a *religion* built around him.
   (That guy was Rocket Richard; the religion is the
   Montreal Canadiens.)
3. Hockey is safely homoerotic for the hetero man.
   Men in this game touch and rub up against one
   another more intensely than the barely legal boys in
   hard-core twink porn, yet straight guys in the stands
   simply *scream* for more. *Woof-uh-licious!*

4. More so than even wrestling, hockey is like a comic book come to life. You've got heroes! Villains! Colorful uniforms! Masks! And show-stopping battles!

5. At any moment during a hockey game, someone might try to punch someone else in the face. I know that's not a sentiment the National Hockey League wants to promote, but here's the worst-kept secret in marketing: The promise of violence puts asses in seats. Why shy away from that? What are the movies that always top the box office? Blockbuster action flicks. Why do we go to action movies? Because we see imagery in promotional materials that shows people or things fighting, exploding, or going very fast. All of our popcorn movies end with giant, explosive showdowns or massive twenty-minute fistfights. Hockey is a mash-up between sports and movies: At any moment, the players on the stage can become so passionate about their performance, they may punch a motherfucker right in the mouth. You don't get fistfights in baseball, basketball, or football, and yet that's rarely trumpeted in the marketing; nobody sells the big three with *"Enjoy these athletic competitions in which there's little threat of true impromptu releases of frustration or physical expressions of general dislike/disapproval!"* There's no need: Most of those athletes understand they're getting paid millions of dollars to play a grown-up version of a kids' game that's ultimately unimportant in the grand scheme of things. But a hockey player knows a higher truth—which is that nothing else in this life will ever matter or be right until they raise a

Stanley Cup. Hockey players skate to the beat of their own drum, and their game is a graceful but aggressive pastime that can elevate to and just as quickly retreat from physical hostilities at the drop of a puck.

Just like life.

We're all hockey players at heart. We're goal-oriented, but it's never easy finding twine because we get hit hard when we rush the net. We take our shots, and the more we shoot, the more precise and dangerous we become. We try to stay out of the scrums, but sometimes we rush into the corners, accepting the fact that even the best players will get penalized from time to time. It doesn't matter what line you're on, you come over the boards and you *contribute*; you produce for the *team*. We assist and we *receive* assistance, but you can't skate every shift, and you can't win alone.

It's an exhausting but exhilarating game, best when played with heart. If you go out there unprepared, you're gonna lose teeth. Actually, with age, you're gonna lose teeth regardless; might as well lose 'em fighting *for* something. It's a fun game, a brutal game, a beautiful game, the fastest game.

But as with all discussions of hockey anywhere, sooner or later, all talk turns to the greatest hockey player who ever lived—an athlete who dominates the top stats of his sport by larger margins than the leaders in all the other sports dominate *their* respective leagues. And as the Wayne Gretzky story unfolded, I was transfixed. Transformed, even. I'd listen to stories told by his father about a boy who would go out of his way to help lesser teammates score goals. I marveled at the symmetry of his seemingly storybook career: how he met his hero Gordie Howe when he was just a boy, and how he'd later skate beside the living legend in the World Hockey Association. My heart would swoon every time they talked about how giving he was with the fans and the press. And my brain exploded when I read the numbers and realized that the greatest hockey player who ever lived—a scoring genius like no other—had more assists on his record than goals. He didn't need to score every time he was near the net with the puck; if you were on the ice with him, Wayne Douglas Gretzky would rather pass the puck to *you*—so *you* could score.

So even though I'd only ever net-minded in street hockey games on the tennis courts of the Highlands Recreation Center and was not (by any reports) the Great One at *anything*, there was something *familiar* about this star center from the fabled Edmonton Oilers—the last dynasty team the NHL has ever known.

He didn't look like a hockey player. He was an average skater, and his slap shot wasn't very powerful. Nobody expected anything much from him, at first glance . . . and that's when he'd hit 'em with *his* game, a game that took folks awhile to understand, because Gretzky saw hockey differently than anybody else. And that was because of a little piece of advice his father gave him.

The story of Wayne Douglas Gretzky reads like the Great Canadian Novel. The firstborn child of Walter and Phyllis Gretzky of Brantford, Ontario, the boy laced up his first pair of skates at age two and scored his first goal by age three, sticking that shit squarely in the five-hole of his beloved Grandma Gretzky as she tended goal in her recliner in the basement between periods of *Hockey Night in Canada*. The boy took to hockey so passionately, his father flooded the backyard, creating a small personal skating rink, where Wayne played and practiced for months each year, augmenting his virtuoso natural ability by aggregating endless hours of ice time.

It was a simple lesson the boy's father taught him, the first rule of hockey, so far as Walter Gretzky was concerned: "Don't go where the puck's been; go where it's *gonna* be."

Puck-chasing was the domain of those who couldn't figure out where the puck would wind up. If you're chasing the puck, you're always a step behind; but if the unpredictable nature of frozen, vulcanized rubber could somehow be counted on to do what *you* thought it might in any given moment during a game, then you wouldn't care what it was doing, you'd only care about what it'd likely do *next*. You'd see the puck where it was but know where the puck was *going* to be in the immediate future. If you know where the puck's gonna be, you're a few strides closer than anybody else on the ice to scooping up the biscuit and putting it in the basket. Knowing where the puck's gonna be doesn't necessarily mean you'll win the game or even score a goal, really . . . but it will certainly give you an edge in a game of tough competitors.

Getting baked and watching these DVDs, I suddenly found a role model in this athlete from Canada whom I began focusing on as a higher power. He was an inspiration, even though he was long retired from the game. This boy from Brantford and his scrappy team of hall-of-famers-in-training became Christ and his apostles to me. Like a recent Alcoholics Anonymous member going whole-hog, I'd whip around chapter and verse from the Book of Gretzky in nearly all conversations, making the hockey legend a phi-losopher demigod of sorts whose father's advice against puck-chasing was now my mantra.

A few emo-bitches tried to take the wind out of my sails by pointing out that, ultimately, Wayne Gretzky—the greatest hockey player who ever lived—was no more than an entertainer. When you remove poetic metaphors, hockey *is* just a kids' game. Some could even argue that being ex-cellent at playing hockey is about as useful and important in the grand scheme of things as being excellent at playing Mo-nopoly. If civilization collapses, the skills of any entertainer mean fuck-all.

But while the center still holds, we love our entertainers— particularly the ones who ply their craft with absolute passion. Wayne Gretzky did that: Number 99 played the game like he was saving mankind from destruction. He was Hockey Jesus. At thirty-eight, I discovered an artist of another sort who did something so utterly useless so incredibly well, and with such vigor and conviction, that you believed the game he was playing actually *mattered* somehow. Suddenly, the Stanley Cup went from being a simple challenge trophy to Christ's own Grail, where your name could be stamped into immortality.

What I do for a living (much like what Wayne Gretzky did for a living) is ultimately unimportant. It will not save lives. It will not stop the planet-killing asteroids, should their time come. It will not change how we survive as a species.

But so long as I pour everything into it as if it *does*

matter? So long as I empty the tank and play the game with pure passion? Then even the mundane elements of a life that will likely end badly can be elevated, elaborated, and celebrated.

I think I encountered Gretzky at the right time—when film suddenly failed to capture my imagination the way it did when I was in my early twenties. In my Gretzky studies, one of the most important aspects of his career biography is the end, when he hung up the skates for good. Here was a man whose every thought for most of his life was hockey oriented. Here was a man known the world over for being synonymous with hockey—whose very name had become interchangeable with the game he played.

And even *he* stopped playing hockey eventually—gracefully, and without much fuss. Wayne Gretzky decided to end his career on his terms, well before his body could ever say, "Fuck you, Gretz," and quit on him. He'd chased his passion and won his dream job, getting paid handsomely to do something he'd have done anyway for free, something he *loved*. And after that was done, he hung up his skates and did something else entirely.

The tough shit we learn from the culture of hockey is that everything ends—even the good shit. *Especially* the good shit. You never know how long you're gonna be on the ice, so it's important to suck the marrow out of every moment in life—because before you know it, the moments become memories, and the to-do remains undone. Nothing gold can stay, Ponyboy—and even the greatest hockey player in the world has to walk away from the game he loves sooner or later. Or, rather, skate away.

But before I skated away from *my* game, I was gonna give 'em a strong third period. I wasn't interested in where the puck was anymore; now I wanted to know where it was *gonna* be.

Wayne Gretzky said, "You miss a hundred percent of the shots you never take." I realized I was just being cute with my puck. It was time to start firing that shit top-shelf.

CHAPTER EIGHT

When the Shit Hit the Fan:

Red State, Part I

Some filmmakers are talented enough to let their work simply speak for itself.

I'm the other guy.

I've always been more P. T. Barnum than P. T. Anderson when it comes to getting a film out there. That's because I was trained by Harvey Weinstein—the slickest salesman since Don Draper.

After Miramax picked up *Clerks* at Sundance 1994, Harvey had Scott and me up to his office for a "Welcome to the family" chitchat. As Scott and I sat across the desk from him, Harvey was approving artwork, looking at a recut scene, fielding power phone calls, and generally multitasking like a cartoon octopus, all while dropping pearls of wisdom on me and Mos. But it was one particular bon mot he'd drop that would define the type of showman I'd become.

"In my experience, the movie doesn't begin and end when the lights go down and the lights come up," Harvey proclaimed, while cracking open another Diet Coke. "If you're really good at your job, the movie begins long before they get to the theater. And if you're a fucking magician? It never ends—even after the credits roll."

It could've just been some bullshit a movie mogul says to kids who're tryin' to make good, but I actually saw his words in practice a few months later when *Clerks* screened at the WorldFest-Houston. After the flick, Mos and I got up and did Q&A—which had developed into more of a slacker joke-fest, as I couldn't take *Clerks* or it's production as seriously as most other filmmakers treated their films at film festival Q&A's. How could I? The flick was ninety minutes full of dick jokes, set in a convenience store.

So while I tried to be informative during the Q&A, I tried more than anything else to be entertaining first and foremost. If someone puts you in front of a crowd with a microphone in your hand, I've always felt it's your duty to give 'em a little bit of a show. Dial it up and snap into performance mode so nobody gets bored or starts to wonder, "Why are they letting this fat guy talk to me?" At that particular Q&A, Mos and I were on fire that evening, regaling the audience with tales of getting the cat to shit on cue. When the laughs were done and the folks were filing out, I overheard a conversation between a pair of exiting audience members: two dudes around my age at the time, maybe a little older. Their exchange went *exactly* like this.

GUY 1: What'd you think of the movie?
GUY 2: I thought it sucked. But the fat guy was *funny*.

Guy 2 didn't dig *Clerks*, and that might've been the end of it. He might've never sampled my wares again. But by simply talking and telling stories about the making of the movie, I'd reached him: He'd now likely try something else I made in the future. The movie hadn't ended when the credits rolled because we kept the experience going. And somehow, it buttressed what'd gone before—which was weak in Guy 2's mind.

That only works, however, if you get 'em in the door in the first place. But how do you get 'em off their couches and into the theaters?

You make a little noise.

As Miramaxateers, we were taught to always use the press to our advantage—manipulate it, even, if you could. Commercials and newspaper ads or billboards for a movie were cost-prohibitive. The press, however? Cheap and voraciously hungry at all times. Lots of inches to fill every day in those newspapers, Harvey'd remind us, pointing out that *someone* had to give 'em something to write about. And with almost *every* Miramax release, he somehow found a way to get people talking, long before the flick was playing anywhere *near* them—without heavy marketing spends in other media. That's because Harvey's marketing campaigns in the mid-'90s weren't based on TV spots: They were based on creating a story around every movie so that there'd be press interest, with or without movie stars.

When *Clerks* went before the Motion Picture Association of America's ratings board in 1994, the flick received a prohibitive NC-17. Normally, this X-rating replacement was reserved for films that depicted sex and adult themes that stopped just shy of penetration. *Clerks* was given the

NC-17 rating solely for the salty dialogue and for concepts that were *discussed*—not even *visualized*. Because we talked about snowballing, sucking thirty-seven dicks, and accidental corpse-fucking, we were grouped with *Henry & June* and *Tie Me Up! Tie Me Down!* Classy company, but those films at least had some nipples in 'em. *Clerks* didn't even have *talk* about breasts, let alone present a tit for audience approval. There's nary a nip-slip in the flick.

Although they were Disney-owned at that point, Harvey still hadn't shaken all of the tricks of the trade that'd built his little company into a now-Disney-owned cinematic juggernaut. So while I saw the NC-17 rating *Clerks* was given as a curse, worried I'd have to eventually make cuts or alter my flick to get an R rating, Harvey saw it as a windfall of publicity. He insisted this was a case of censorship, this rating, so he hired *Reversal of Fortune* legal mind and O. J. defender Alan Dershowitz to rep the film against the Motion Picture Association of America.

It had all the subtlety of using a bazooka to pitch Wiffle Balls, but it was incredibly effective: There was an instant slew of media coverage as Harvey spun the voluntary ratings system into a battleground for freedom of speech. Scott and I sat with Dershowitz at a press conference, where the legendary lawyer insisted his teenage kid should be able to watch *Clerks* as a precautionary tale *without* needing permission from a parent to do so, because the moral of the story he wanted his son to be able to learn was so essential: Go to college or you'll end up like these two losers behind convenience-store counters.

When the time came to actually face the MPAA and argue

for an R over the NC-17, we were repped by a Miramax lawyer. Alan Dershowitz, it seemed, only had been retained for that press conference to kick-start publicity. But pay him to actually be a lawyer on the film's behalf? Why bother! All that freedom of speech and anticensorship talk was hot air, as Harvey told us that if the MPAA upheld the NC-17, then editing out the objectionable material was going to be our next step. We'd take on the establishment to a point, but only for the noise it created. Mercifully, even without the Dersh, we got the MPAA appeals board to overturn the rating that day, without having to make a single cut.

I'd asked Harvey if the Dershowitz stunt was expensive, and he responded proudly that, all in all, the entire process cost less than the airing of one television spot in primetime on network TV. *Clerks* was being buzzed about in media circles that it likely would not have been discussed in otherwise were it not for the faux First Amendment circus Harvey created. *Get the movie noticed* was the Miramax mantra. *Shoot it out of a fucking cannon if you gotta, but get the movie noticed. By any means necessary.*

At Warner Bros., when it came to opening a movie, things were decidedly different. They're a publicly traded entertainment conglomerate. They have gobs of money to make *and* open movies. And they don't rely on blind items in the press or scandals that land the flicks on the op-ed pages of the newspapers; they just buy full-page ads for posters of their movies. There's no shuck and jive; they simply carpet-bomb a movie into the public consciousness through every media platform that's legal. When their flicks are in theaters, you may not choose to see them but you will *know* they are there. It was quite a thing to behold and so completely foreign to me, as well as counter to everything I'd been taught about film exhibition by Harvey.

Post–*Cop Out*, Warner Bros. started talking to me about directing more films at the studio. I'd proven that I could weather a pretty bad storm and still bring a picture in under budget, and for that, I'd earned a place at the WB table—my reward for surviving Willis. Granted, these weren't films I'd *write* and direct: WB had scripts they wanted me to make first, so I'd just be a director for hire on their projects. But if any of those flicks worked really well at the box office, I could always try to guilt them into letting me direct something *I'd* written.

I was entering a new stage in my career that I never imagined I'd get to: groomed to be a studio filmmaker. I wouldn't be expected to find the money or beg the crew to perform for less than standard wages. I wouldn't be expected to sleep three hours a night in production, and there'd be second and third units running simultaneously, each with their own director and crew. I could pay the cast what they were worth instead of asking them to take cuts. I could *host* the movie, be the guy who makes everyone comfortable, basically overseeing the show.

I was set to say yes when I remembered a panel from Frank Miller's seminal graphic novel *The Dark Knight Returns.* Long retired from being Batman, Bruce Wayne races a Formula One car and nearly wrecks it. As the car's about to eat it, Wayne's internal monologue is beautiful: *"This would be a good death . . ."*

And while it's not blowing up in a fiery car wreck, hosting movies for a living would've been a good death for me: I could've spent the rest of my life hiding from myself inside a movie studio, getting paid a king's ransom to make pretend with someone else's stories. What's the difference, right? A movie's a movie.

Then I remembered the follow-up line Miller penned for the once and future Batman that appears in the very next panel, as he jerks the wheel and changes the course of his destiny . . .

"But not good enough."

And suddenly, there was that nagging, stupid voice in my head again—the one that whispers, "Never take the path of least resistance; because nothing worthwhile is easy." I recalled my Gretzky training: not the training I actually did with Gretzky himself (that'd be zero), but instead, all the time I put into reading about and studying this paragon of character and sportsmanship. Did I want to rush into the scrum again with everyone else? Or did I want to figure out where the puck was *going* to be?

And from my position on the ice, it looked like the puck was traveling someplace indie as fuck.

So I thanked Jeff Robinov and all the good folks I worked with at Warner Bros. during *Cop Out*—none of them the art-destroying studio Stormtroopers with which Miramax had filled our heads—and I started looking for *Red State* money instead.

Red State had been a long-gestating experimental flick I'd been threatening to make for a few years. Here was a windmill at which to tilt: a script I'd written years prior that was conceived about as far from the path of least resistance as one could get. It was a dark little comic book of a movie about three boys who go into the woods to find sex, and instead find God.

As I was writing *Red State*, any time I felt like I knew where the plot was going I assumed that meant the audience would've figured it out as well. So instead of writing a traditional narrative in a three-act structure, I opted to go for a genre mash-up movie that's impossible to get ahead of: Whenever I knew where the story was going, I simply switched gears and jumped off that track altogether. As much as I love *Zack and Miri Make a Porno*, you know the main characters are gonna fall for each other; it's predictable. I wanted to make a flick that was as unpredictable as a terrier on heroin—a fever-pitched funhouse nightmare with lots of uncomfortable gallows humor and no clear path out, where the bad guys didn't wear hockey masks or carry chainsaws; they protested at funerals. My models were *Race with the Devil*—a 1970s Peter Fonda picture about a weekend getaway spoiled by satanic sacrifice—as well as the normalcy of the geriatrics next door in *Rosemary's Baby*. Compound that with lots of Tarantino, pile on some Coen brothers, and let it simmer for five years, while everyone passes on financing it.

While I was waiting for Seth Rogen to say yay or nay to playing the lead in *Zack and Miri Make a Porno*, I wrote *Red State* in three days and submitted it to the Weinstein Company—looking for essentially the same *Clerks II* budget. But both Harvey and Bob passed on *Red State*—the first time that'd ever happened in my Weinstein tenure. It was confusing as fuck since the script was classic Miramax: weird, outside the box, actor bait, inexpensive, and ballsy.

The problem was that we weren't at Miramax anymore.

By the time Harvey and Bob got divorced from Disney, Miramax was no longer the little distribution company that released Hal Hartley's *The Unbelievable Truth;* it was making expensive, studio-size movies like *The Aviator*. When they opened the doors at the Weinstein Company, the mantra was simple: sure things. With Harvey insisting it was a horror movie that Bob should make, and Bob insisting it was an art-house flick Harvey should make, if *Red State* was ever going to get made, it'd have to happen *without* the Weinsteins.

It'd have to happen without my longtime producer Scott Mosier as well. After helping me tell my stories for over a decade, Mos was on a vision quest to tell his *own* stories. So I turned to my friend and former fellow Miramax mendicant Jon Gordon and asked him to produce *Red State*. Jon had been Harvey Weinstein's assistant when Miramax picked up *Clerks* in 1994 and was largely responsible for every flick I'd ever made at Miramax after that, since he was the guy who signed my production company, View Askew, to a first-look, overall deal at the emerging mini-major. We became fast friends, bound by our belief in the cinematic Camelot that was our home. Jon was another dyed-in-the-wool Miramaxkateer who'd started interning with Harvey while in school, and went to work at Miramax the day he graduated from college. The two of us saw ourselves as Defenders of the Faith, hopelessly devoted to the Miramax indie ethos.

But during the post-Disney-divorce great migration to The WC, rather than watch Miramax Redux become a mainstream-encrusted mockery of itself, Jon scored a studio gig running Universal for a while—a clear indicator that Camelot was no more. When he left Universal, he came to the same conclusion at which many of us who were educated in the Weinsteinian ways eventually arrive: *Harvey raised me to do this myself.* Sooner or later, like Jason Bourne, your training kicks in . . . and motherfuckers start getting punched in the mush.

Jon introduced me to Elyse Seiden, a family friend who'd read and loved the *Red State* script. Elyse introduced us to a businessman in New York City who wanted to invest in a film. At our first meeting, I asked him if he'd read the script for *Red State*. He said that wouldn't be necessary.

"I saw your name on a movie with Bruce Willis in it, so I know you're legit."

Then he wrote me a two-and-a-half-million-dollar check—half the budget of *Red State*. I felt like Andy Dufresne: After crawling through the river of shit that was working with Bruce Willis, I had emerged from Shawshank's guts and fallen into a stream of revenue. Years after writing *Red*, we were finally gonna start shooting.

I say this with no hint of irony: Shooting *Red State* was a religious experience. It was one of those shows that's more like summer camp. The cast and crew were amazingly patient and brought their A-games, all working for scale wages or less. I was surrounded by new faces in front of and behind the cameras, but by the end of the first day, we were bonded for life as family. That's the way it goes on an indie film: In lieu of having money, people have love for what they're working on as well as for the people they're working with to bring the flicks to life.

John Goodman is both America's dad in *Roseanne* and America's best friend in *The Big Lebowski*. I'd been a fan since his panda-bear turn in David Byrne's *True Stories*.

Goodman improved any movie he was in, so I wanted him to play my conflicted ATF agent Joe Keenan. And here's what a good man Goodman is: He didn't get paid much at all. If I told you what we paid John Goodman to be in *Red State*, you'd find me and kick me in the balls, screaming, "He's a treasure! An American treasure, you fat prick!"

We scored his *Treme* costar first, however, when Melissa Leo from *Frozen River* read the script and signed on to play Sara, Abin Cooper's daughter. By the time we rolled cameras months later, Melissa was already receiving lots of Oscar buzz for her performance in *The Fighter*. When she won the Best Supporting Actress Oscar early the next year, she broke new ground for the potty-mouthed set by uttering "fuck" during her acceptance speech.

One of my biggest regrets in life will always be not seeing Michael Parks say "fuck" while *he* collects awards for his work in *Red State*. Parks put the spine, balls, brain, and soul into the flick, giving a performance so otherworldly and next generation that you'd imagine they started engraving his name on closets full of awards. Parks knocked that shit out of the park.

Jon and I made Elyse a producer and formed a new production company, calling it the Harvey Boys in honor of the man who taught us everything we knew about filmmaking, distribution, self-marketing, and independence. We imagined our sensei would eventually see the film Jon and I made all on our own, using the lessons he taught us years prior, and we dreamed he would say to us, "This movie's everything that we used to do at Miramax! You boys were paying attention! I'm so proud!"

That's what I felt in my head and heart. I was forty years old, but this "adult film," as I called it, was gonna be my movie-biz bar mitzvah (or bar SMitzvah, if you will).

But on day four on the set of *Red State*, while watching all the beautiful people in my cast and on my crew pull together to make this ugly little story, I started thinking about how the marketing dollars spent to open this film eventually would be four or five times the amount that all the generous filmmakers on my cast and crew (who took drastic cuts in salary to work on the flick) ever had to work with in their departments to actually *make* the flick. I was asking the cast and crew to eat gristle when, postpurchase, the choice cuts would go elsewhere.

What would even ultimately happen to our love child *Red State*? We all hoped someone would eventually buy the film when it was finished, but how much would they buy it *for*? *Happy, Texas* sold for $10 million at Sundance back in 1999, but those days were long gone. *Buried* sold for $6 million in 2010, but that had Ryan Reynolds in it.

And if it got bought, what would happen *then*? Like, let's say Lionsgate picked up *Red State*. Lionsgate spends an almost-standard $20 mil to open any flick (which is lower than the industry norm; LG is actually one of the more frugal studios, spending less on marketing than the majors). So now, my flick doesn't cost $4 million anymore, it costs $24 million. It's gotta make $24 million to break even and start seeing profit. But the studio/distributor doesn't get *all* that box office, so assume the studio only gets back *half* of that announced box-office figure. Suddenly my little four-million-dollar movie has to make $50 million *JUST TO BREAK EVEN*. Like . . . what *happened*? Instead of spending all that money trying to make the movie, the money is spent on trying to convince people to come see your shit.

And where's that $20 million go? It's called "P&A"—prints and advertising. But the print portion of that equation—physically creating the reels of film that make up the movie—is pretty low: It costs between two and three grand to make five or six reels of a motion picture (the costs of a digital print are lower). So let's say you make a thousand prints: You're looking at $2 to $3 million dollars.

That leaves $17 to $18 million of the P&A to account for. Where's *that* big chunk gonna go? Try TV spots, full-page ads in newspapers and magazines, billboards and bus-stop posters, thousands of mini-prints of trailers, press junkets, airfare . . .

But this far along in his career, why would you even *spend* money to market *any* Kevin Smith flick to the casual or ardent View Askew/*SModcast*/Kevin Smith fan? What would be the point? If you're remotely a fan of that shit, you're already aware of whatever it is we've got coming, because Fatty McNoFly never shuts up about it. And he's had lots of practice.

In 1995, we opened ViewAskew.com—a Web site that consisted of lots of *Clerks* and *Mallrats* jpegs, sound bytes, and mpegs, with a shit-ton of text by me, and perhaps the most important feature, and the one that would change my life: The View Askew Message Board.

On that message board, back in 1995, I was essentially tweeting. We called it *posting* in those days, but it's the same idea: Someone who liked what I did for a living could ask me questions and I could respond. It was direct contact with the audience, along the lines of a postscreening Q&A.

Back then, Peter Jackson and I were the only filmmakers treating the Web seriously, responding to folks who dug our stuff. And while Peter Jackson eventually concentrated less on the Web and more on wowing audiences with his Oscar-winning epics, I opted to concentrate more on the Web, wowing audiences with my creepy omnipresence and inability to answer questions in less than two sentences.

By *Dogma*, we started to realize I had a deadhead thing going on with my audience. There were four films, interconnected, that lots of folks caught up with on video. And the folks who'd notice and dig on the interconnectivity were mostly Web-babies: the generation born online. They'd hear you could talk to the fat guy who made those flicks and those commentary tracks right at his Web site, where he holds court, talks shop, and hawks merchandise. They'd find out it was not only true, but that the *Clerks* guy would also throw mini film festivals of flicks he and his friends made; or that you could go to his comic book store and see people from his movies. And it was no coincidence that the box office for the flicks grew exponentially as the board membership jumped into five and six figures.

But rather than be embraced and appreciated by the powers that be, that audience was always dismissed or minimized. I'd see trailers or posters for our flicks that didn't resemble the movies at all, and any time I said, "My audience is gonna hate this . . . ," I was told, "Your audience is already coming, no matter what. We're reaching *beyond* your audience this time . . ."

All the marketing materials, you see, had tested positively in a mall: Studios pay marketing firms to bring movie trailers to malls and ask set demographics to yay 'em or nay 'em. That's about $5 to $10 thousand, depending on how long you want to grab samples—samples that don't include actual fans, who always reported being turned away for answering affirmatively to the question, "Have you ever seen *Clerks, Mallrats,* or *Chasing Amy*?"

Going after that mythical new audience was always costly, too. Millions spent trying to convince people who wouldn't like my shit anyway, to pay to come see it. Millions spent to beg a disinterested crowd to join our party. And any time I spoke about my audience, I'd get the pat on the head: "That's cute, Kevin." The intent to bring me into the mainstream was always flattering, but let's be honest: What I do in film (or anywhere, for that matter) isn't *for* everybody. For lots of folks, my flicks are about cuss words and inept framing; for lots of others, they're the stories of their lives.

It just started to gnaw at me. Many cats were breaking their backs to see us hit an ambitiously low budget cap, but whoever bought the flick would then give people who never worked on the movie way *more* money to simply sell it to an audience that didn't care about or want it. And after nine flicks, I just couldn't see my way clear to doing it the old way one more time; not with a budget as low as *ours*. Four million bucks? We could make that make, *without* all the crazy marketing spending.

The first person I spoke to about the idea was Jon Gordon. I'd said, "What do you think about self-distribution? Like . . . *not* selling the flick when we're done."

It was the next day when Jon and I rejoined the conversation that we started figuring out what we had at our disposal. The idea was to combine everything I'd learned over the years to work together, all at once: nearly two decades in filmmaking, seventeen years of standing on a stage and answering questions with as many cock jokes as I could muster, and almost four years of heavy-duty podcasting. We could combine all three by taking the movie out ourselves, on a cross-country tour.

The idea to control our own destiny came not just from years of watching Harvey and Bob work, but also from the music business. When Trent Reznor and Radiohead unplugged from their labels and began dealing *directly* with their audience, they started a fire that would ultimately help change the music business forever, putting control back into the hands of the artist. But what happens if you try it in *film*? The musicians started a fire; this filmmaker wanted to see if the fire would rise.

When we rolled cameras on *Red State*, Sundance hadn't been part of the plan. When we were looking at an early August start, there was a good chance we could edit the film into something showable by the Sundance submission deadline. But it took longer to close on all the financing with our New York and Canadian financiers than we'd planned, so we pushed our start date by a month and change. At that point, we assumed we wouldn't be ready to submit the flick to Sundance in time. The thought, then, was to instead aim for a Cannes debut in May.

I not only write and direct the movies I make, I edit them as well. In production, whenever I'm not on set, I'm in the editing room, chop-sockying the flick together on my Avid. On *Red*, I spent the entire shoot editing the flick every night and during any free time I had during the shoot days. Every day at wrap, DP Dave Klein, AD Adam Druxman, and I would discuss the next morning's work: the first shot of the day as well as the rest of the set-ups for that scene. Then, in the morning at call-time, the crew would set up without me, leaving more time for me to edit, hitting the set at the last possible second before we'd roll on the first take. The beauty of this? After the first take (or sometimes before), I could gather the cast and crew around the monitor and show them the actual flick, edited—which had only been shot the day before. And watching the movie take shape as something recognizable (an edited film) always gets the blood going and keeps the cast and crew enthused. The film, at that point, is no longer theoretical—it's real as raincoats.

So at the wrap party at my house—about a day and change after the final shot on *Red State*—the cast and crew were able to watch the same cut of *Red State* we'd eventually screen at Sundance. Over two hundred people were packed into my living room, including Michael Parks, watching the flick and enjoying the love for him and his performance in the room, with one of his tea-cup dogs in his jacket. We were unexpectedly finished enough with the film to show the flick to the Sundance folks before the submission deadline. John Cooper, Trevor Groth, and the rest of the Sundance kids who make up the selection committee saw the flick and gave us the acceptance nod, and suddenly, seventeen years after the fact, I was going to be returning to Sundance—the film festival where I started my career. There, Jon and I would announce our intentions to self-distribute *Red State*.

After Miramax picked up *Clerks* at Sundance 1994, from February forward Scott and I took the movie from film festival to film festival, college screening to college screening, getting the word out *well* in advance of our October 19 opening. But who'd pay for all that *this* time? Back then, Miramax would foot the bills. Any awareness screenings we were gonna do with *Red State* were gonna have to be paid for. We didn't have a studio or a distributor with deep pockets this time: It was just *us*.

Then my Weinstein training kicked in.

Between films, you can normally find me touring the country, doing Q&A wherever anybody has set up a microphone and gathered a couple of warm bodies. For the last two years, I have stepped up my live gigs considerably, including taking live podcasts on the road—so much so that, lately, I've earned more just being me on a stage somewhere than I have for directing film. And since I did *Red State* for no money, I was going to spend the next few months touring the country again, earning by speaking.

I started thinking about hitching up a screening in the afternoon of any show I was doing—so you could pay to see *Red State* first if you wanted, before seeing my separate Q&A show later that night. Then we figured, just *combine* the two: movie *then* Q&A—all at one price. And rather than increase the price of what folks were already paying to see me do, Q&A *without* the movie, we add on the movie that evening, essentially "for free."

Together with Jeff Hyman (the man who puts my fat ass on stages across the world), Jon Gordon and I plotted a *Red State* tour that could run from March to April. We'd hit a bunch of major markets where I'd previously sold out Q&A shows, knowing we had built-in audiences to vend to. And while profit is always the overall goal, we devised a theater rental schedule that'd allow us, more important, to not *spend* anything in advance, using advance ticket sales to pay for each venue. This is not inspired or new; this is called *four-walling*: renting the theater and selling the seats yourself. We chose Boston's Wilbur Theatre, Chicago's Harris Theater, the Michigan Theater in Ann Arbor, Clowes Memorial Hall in Indianapolis, the Midland Theatre in Kansas City, Clark State PAC in Ohio, the Warner Theatre in D.C., the Paramount Theatre in Denver, the Paramount in Austin, the Cobb Energy Performing Arts Centre in Atlanta, McCaw Hall in Seattle, and the Wiltern in Los Angeles. Eventually, we'd add Minnesota and New Orleans venues, but we knew we had to kick off the tour in New York City at Carnegie Hall. Sadly, it was booked for the date we wanted to launch the tour. But Jon's a native New Yorker and I'm from across the river in Jersey, so since we couldn't get *that* iconic New York City theater, we opted for another—the one where, ironically, I'd attended the *Live Free or Die Hard* premiere with Bruce Willis years prior.

Radio City Music Hall is a 6,000 seater that I knew we could never sell out in a month with no advertising spend. But that didn't matter: It was the idea that two fucking movie dorks like me and Jon could actually rent Radio City Music Hall *at all* to show our weird little flick in that made it sound fun. There's a short list of movies that have actually played at Radio City in the past twenty years, and we'd be on it. The moment Jon compared it to Spicoli getting Van Halen to play his birthday party, I was *in*.

It's a giant barn, but thankfully all we had to sell were 1,700 seats: That was the break-even point—the amount of tickets we had to sell so the cost of our rental of Radio City that night would be covered. After that, every ticket sold would be gravy. The rest of the shows across the country were all under half the size of Radio City, so our break-even numbers everywhere else were far lower. But the moment we hit 1,700 tickets sold at Radio City, I assure you—we uncorked champagne and unclenched our assholes.

But in order to get *Red State* out into the world without spending money, we needed to launch as high profile as we could. We had to shoot out of a *cannon*. We needed to make a big splash in the adult pool, along the order of hiring Alan Dershowitz to rep *Clerks* at a press conference about censorship. We'd named our company the Harvey Boys, so we asked ourselves not "What would Harvey *do*?" but rather "What would Harvey *have done* back in the early '90s?" And suddenly, we knew:

He'd Barnum and Bailey the shit out of it.

In November, before we knew whether or not we'd gotten into Sundance, I gave an e-mail interview with SlashFilm.com about eventually retiring. In it, I included a line that I knew would get picked up by a lot of online news sites . . .

"Here's something that's not so much news as my stated intentions for *Red State*: If it gets into Sundance, my plan is to pick the *Red State* distributor right there—IN THE ROOM—auction style."

Within 24 hours, lots of sites were writing that I intended to auction *Red State* right after the screening, to the highest bidder. But look at how carefully I worded it: I didn't say anything about selling the film. Yet in every article and news item generated from that SlashFilm story, that's what was extrapolated. The press literally put words into my mouth. It wasn't exactly what we were hoping for: It was even *better.*

After that, we lit the match: We released the teaser trailer for *Red State* online. This was the least Kevin Smith–looking flick I'd ever made, so it created lots of chatter. And mind you, it was following *Cop Out*—so already, the boring "Is Kevin Smith back?" question started popping up in blogs and online articles linking to the trailer. I was about to embark on the "We Forgive You" tour yet again.

I'd first dealt with it on *Chasing Amy*—the patronizing omniquestions every journalist you speak with gets to ask so that you can sell your flick: *"So, this movie is good, but what happened with that last one?"* Or some of that *"Now that you've learned your lesson . . ."* kinda shit. Ugh . . . so fucking gross. They want you to be contrite—to apologize for a movie they didn't like, in exchange for which they'll tell people about your new, "good" movie. They all work from the same *Behind the Music* three-act structure: You did well, you fucked up, now you're back. Celebrities can be boring enough without the help of an even less imaginative profiler. They criticize you for making a movie that's been done before, yet they write the same, lame three-act profiles over and over again.

It'd irritated me whenever I'd see Ben Affleck do an interview for *The Town*: In each sit-down or profile, they'd bring up Bennifer and his string of flops. Before they'd give him his props, they'd cut him down to size—right in front of his face—and tell him his previous work was shit. And in order to get the coverage needed for his new flick, Ben had to sit there and grin through it.

And here I was, about to dance this tired dance yet again. "*Chasing Amy* made up for *Mallrats*," the locusts chirped. "*Clerks II* made up for *Jersey Girl*." And I was about to face another round of that sickening condescension: "*Red State* makes up for *Cop Out*," would say the people who never risk anything. And if I hadn't done it twice already in my career, maybe I'd have been able to slap that grin on my face one more time and bare their condescension so I could sell my film. But Dad died screaming. Life's too short. And there's more than one way to skin a cock.

And I knew the cocks would scream for my blood when I'd announce on the Sundance stage a month or so later that the Harvey Boys were buying the movie themselves, the auction they'd inferred I was holding, merely a figment of their imagination. We needed their ire: It was free ink. I'd been in the business long enough to realize that if they were writing about *Red State*, good or bad, it was free ink to the mainstream crowd, that wouldn't affect the core audience one way the other.

But had I known we'd eventually be joined by marketing partners at our *Red State* debut, I wouldn't have needed the theatrics of the phantom auction to launch the *Red State* USA Tour at the fest. I could've just written, "If we get into Sundance, expect a holy war."

CHAPTER NINE

Holy Shit:

Red State, Part II

Most folks know the Phelps family of the Westboro Baptist Church as the shiny, happy *God Hates Fags* people. They're a family church of fewer than fifty members from Topeka, Kansas, who show up at funerals of AIDS victims, fallen soldiers, or high-profile celebrities, brandishing placards and signs indicating God's displeasure with lots of shit.

The villainous religious extremists in *Red State* are satires of mini-churches like Westboro, but with a ridiculous amount of guns thrown in. In an interview I'd given in the UK years prior, I name-checked Fred Phelps as the model for my bad guy. Since then, the family seemed morbidly curious about my flick, and kind of in love with my fat ass.

They'd even protested me back in March of 2010, when I'd played the Midland Theatre in Kansas City. In advance of my arrival, they issued a Bible-inflected, jeremiad of a press release deeming me a "fag-enabler" who's leading his audience to Hell, and announced their intent to protest outside of my Q&A show.

At that protest, Westboro didn't wave a single protest sign that had anything to do with me: there were no **GOD HATES FATS** placards. They did, however, take issue with the Easter Bunny, which they also depicted as having anal sex with a stick-figure man, surrounded by a *Ghostbusters* "NO" circle and line.

Since then, I'd hear from the Phelps clan from time to time via social media. Fred Phelps's granddaughter, Megan Phelps-Roper, would tweet the fuck out of me, talking fire and brimstone. I'd tweet her back stuff like, "Megs, my wife says that if it'll save you from that cult, we can all have a three-way together."

Shortly before Sundance, Westboro issued a press release announcing their intentions to picket the Sundance *Red State* debut in Park City. No strangers to the road, the Phelps clan log lots of air miles as they crisscross the country in an effort to hold up signs at funerals, generally making everyone's day a little more shitty. Without even seeing it, they knew what *Red State* really was: my cinematic version of holding up a shitty sign at *them*. Why wait for a funeral? Remind them in *life* how ridiculous they are by painting 'em with a satiric brush at twenty-four frames per second. Pull the monster's teeth out, paint them like clowns, and throw 'em up on the big screen so everyone can point and laugh. Credits.

And here they were, crashing our Sundance party. Jon and I wasted no time in releasing our own press release . . .

FOR IMMEDIATE RELEASE:
THE HARVEY BOYS WILL PICKET
THE WESTBORO BAPTIST CHURCH PICKET
OF THE SCREENING OF "RED STATE"
AT THE ECCLES THEATRE,
SUNDAY, JANUARY 23rd, FROM 6:00–6:30 PM

Los Angeles, CA—January 19, 2011- Here are the facts: (1) The Westboro Baptist Church are haters of Biblical proportions! "Thou shalt not hate thy brother in thine heart: thou shalt in any wise rebuke thy neighbour, & not suffer sin upon him." (Lev 19:17) (2) The WBC's punishment in Hell for their hatred will be administered by the very Jesus they blaspheme daily. ". . . he shall be tormented with fire & brimstone in the presence of the holy angels, & in the presence of the Lamb: & the smoke of their torment ascendeth up forever & ever: & they have no rest day nor night." (Rev 14:10-11)

The Harvey Boys are seeking the aid of the Mighty Thor, hoping he'll lay down his hammer and instead pick up a protest sign on our behalf, in a Park City battle of the mega-gods! If he's in re-shoots, we'll be reaching out to Sigourney Weaver to channel Zuul on our behalf. If she's not at Sundance this year, we'll start praying to Krom. And if you don't help us, Krom? Then to hell witchoo.

For thirty minutes of fun-filled photo-opportunities, the Harvey Boys will peacefully counter-protest the WBC Eccles Theater Protest. All are welcome. Wear YOUR dopey sentiments

nobody gives a shit about on a sign of your own
making, as you stand shoulder-to-shoulder with the
folks who've mastered the art of writing utter horseshit on cardboard! BYOS (Bring Your Own Sign)

The scoffing and the mocking will begin sharply
at 6pm. Remember: this is a PEACEFUL protest.
The only venom you bring is printed on a placard,
your only weapon: wit. "Woe unto them that call
evil good, and good evil; that put darkness for light,
and light for darkness . . ." (Isa 5:20)

GOD DOESN'T HATE FAGS OR ANY-
BODY ELSE FOR THAT MATTER. GOD SAVES!
THEN, GOD PASSES IT TO GRETZKY—WHO
ROOFS THAT SHIT, TOP-SHELF! THEN GOD
AND GRETZKY HIGH FIVE & BELLY-BUMP,
CELEBRATING THEIR HOCKEY PROWESS.
AND NEVER ONCE DO THEY GIVE A SHIT
IF ANYBODY'S GAY OR NOT.

The Harvey Boys

We had a crew at Sundance, staying in a rented condo:
me, my wife, Jen, my assistant, Meghan, and her man,
Alan, Mewes and his wife, Jordan, Zack Knudsen and Joey
Figueroa (who were shooting the behind-the-scenes stuff),
Tim Isenman (who was handcuffed to the print), the flick's
spiritual godfather, Malcolm Ingram, and Clovis Scott—our
intrepid bus driver. With all the touring and road shows I'd
been doing, I'd bought my own bus: a used Prevost that was
in pretty cherry condition. It's brown like our dachshund,
Shecky, so we named it the Sheckladore.

The night before the Sundance debut, our entire crew

was sprawled out across the rental condo's floors with markers and cardboard, making ridiculous protest signs to combat Westboro's many GOD HATES FAGS placards.

— Thor Hates Straights

— God Hates Critics

— Down with Mutants

— God Hates Rainy Days and Mondays

— God Loves Mewes's Cock

— God Hates Phelps—Except Megan. God Thinks She's Hot.

— God Loves, Man Kills

Malcolm carried my favorite sign by far—one I suggested only he can make and carry into battle with these Holy Rollers.

"Their entire campaign is predicated on three words: GOD—HATES—FAGS," I explained to Malcolm, who is gay as the day is long. "We counter with three words of our own, packed with more power and truth than *their* tired three words, and you hold a sign that reads DICK—TASTES—YUMMY."

Considering this entire free-for-all was all just a twenty-first century rendition of hiring Alan Dershowitz to show up at a press conference for the *Clerks* ratings battle, naturally, Jon and I invited Harvey and Bob to the premiere screening. We were trying to make the Miramaxiest non-Miramax movie ever made, under a production company banner we named after the man. The bar SMitzvah would happen soon, and both Jon and I would be men in our hero's eyes.

Then, a week before the fest, Jon received an invite to a party Harvey would be hosting at Sundance . . . at the same time as our screening.

The Jets were involved in an important AFC title show-down, so Harvey's party was a football-watching shindig, thrown with a billionaire buddy at the posh Stein Eriksen Lodge at the top of the mountain in Park City, where corporate muckety-mucks could gather and watch the game. About two hours before the screening, we got a call from Sundance head John Cooper, who told us that Harvey had phoned him, asking what could be done about moving the *Red State* screening, maybe starting it *after* the Jets game. Cooper told him that moving the start time of our film wasn't possible, as there were over a thousand people lining up to see the flick at the start time that'd been established a month prior.

So then Harvey called Jon Gordon, telling him to stall the screening so everyone at the party could watch the rest of the Jets game.

Not even *asking*; flat-out *telling*.

The guy we named our company after wanted us to delay the debut screening of our flick at a film festival, just so he could watch a fucking football game.

We told him not to come. If it was such a hassle for a major film distributor to go to a film festival to see a film made by two of his biggest supporters, please—enjoy your football party.

Our crude crusaders loaded up onto the bus and headed over to the Eccles Theatre, which was housed in a high school in Park City. When we got to the theater, it was already a melee: Four Phelpses were given an area from which to protest, surrounded by more lights and cameras than I'd seen since the days of shooting *Jersey Girl* at the height of Bennifermania. But better than the image of church vs.

fourth estate was what was lined up beyond them: kids from the high school had taken our call to arms seriously and created their *own* antiprotest signs—a hilarious collection of innocent inanery aimed at the fucking Phelps Yelps bunch. Signs that read "GOD HATES SIGNS," or my all-time favorite protest placard of 2011—"GOD HATES THAT THERE WERE ONLY 2 SEASONS OF PUSHING DAISIES!" As the Phelps clan sang God Hates America (their fundamentalist Weird Al Yankovic–like cover of "God Bless America"), the Park City Protest Kids sang Lady Gaga songs back at them.

The day of the screening, I auctioned off a pair of seats online for a thousand bucks, which we donated to the Sundance Institute. They were the last two seats available anywhere near the Eccles; the flick had become such a hot ticket. We eliminated our press screenings, so there were only two chances to see *Red State* at Sundance—which really irritated the fuck out of a bunch of people who wrote shitty things about me and my last flick. The line to get into the theater was massive, but the Phelps counter-protest circus was almost like a perfect preshow, so folks were kept entertained while they waited—kinda like the monitors with clips you watch while in line for the Simpsons ride at Universal Studios.

Because of the antics outside, the screening was starting late. I was backstage, getting ready to intro the screening, nervous as hell, when Jason finds me and says, "Harvey's here and he wants to come backstage to see you."

I knew Harvey wasn't there for moral support; he just wanted props for showing up at all. And I was in pregame at that point, steeling myself for what was going to be a career-changing (some would write career-destroying) night. I said, "Keep him away, please."

When I got up on stage to intro the film, I kept things light.

"Sorry we're running late," I began. "My family came and they were out in the parking lot, holding up signs."

I introduced my producers, Jon Gordon and Elyse Seiden. It was really cool for Elyse to be on a Sundance stage as the producer of a film because she'd been working the ticket booth at the previous year's Sundance. I told the crowd we'd started shooting September 21, 2010—so, essentially, from first shot in production to our Sundance debut, it'd only been a whirlwind four months. Then, I hit 'em with the joke I'd beat into the ground for the rest of the year, everywhere we showed the flick . . .

"Ladies and gentlemen, *Red State* is not a comedy, like *Clerks* and *Mallrats*. It's a horror movie—like *Jersey Girl*."

With that, I sat in the back of the Eccles Theatre, right by the door, watching the Little Movie That Could start its long chug up the hill. I'm enjoying the fuck out of the first public exhibition of *Red State* at one of the world's most renowned film festivals, where only seventeen years prior I'd debuted my *first* feature—a film Harvey eventually bought and released through Miramax. I'd returned to the two roads, diverging in a yellow wood. Last time, I took the path everyone takes. This time, I was gonna try the road less traveled to see if it made any difference.

About seven minutes into the screening, I hear the unmistakably boisterous baritone of Harvey Weinstein, and he was *not* using his inside voice. I pushed the door curtain to the side and I saw Harvey in the lobby, talking at his assistant at full volume, barking about the Jets game and what the score was. You know what kind of message that sends, when the biggest name in indie film is at your screening *not* watching the movie?

I was flabbergasted. This was the man who taught me that every screening room deserves churchlike reverence while the movie's playing. You *never* talk during *any* screening, in the theater or in the lobby—that's what Harvey instilled in us back in the day. And here he was, committing a mortal cinematic sin . . . at a Harvey Boys screening.

Although I was outraged, I did nothing. I told myself, "Without this man, I wouldn't even be here right now. Let it go . . ."

I returned to my seat against the back wall of the theater, beside the curtain door. After a minute, the loud-ass talking started again, as Harvey told his assistant to make sure some muckety-muck didn't leave the party—that he'd be back soon.

I told myself, "Everything you have in this life you've got because of Harvey Weinstein. Let it go . . ."

And then he got louder. So loud that he was competing with the movie. That's when I suddenly both grew up *and* grew a set of balls.

I pulled the curtain to the side and whisper-shouted, "*Hey!*"

Harvey looked over at me. With fire in my eyes and in my belly, I called out to him, "*Shut the fuck up!*"

The look of surprise on his face was quickly replaced by anger when I added, "Yeah, shut the fuck up. I would *never* do this to you. I would never come to one of your screenings and act like an asshole. Shut the fuck up!"

The expression on his face was one I'd never been on the receiving end of but had often heard about from others who'd gotten into it with Harvey Weinstein. He looked like he was gonna come over and punch me, so I closed the curtain and sat back down, terrified—waiting for Harvey Scissorhands to come tearing through the cloth, seeking to bloody my face to the (Mira)max.

And nothing happened. After a beat, I opened up the curtain to look again, half expecting to take a fist to the chin. But Harvey was gone. He took off. Now that I think about it, it was the last time we spoke.

About an hour later, I got up onstage carrying a hockey stick:

A week before the festival, in conversation with Malcolm, I'd had the notion of having a powerful totem in my hands—something that would give me the courage and strength I'd need in order to jump up there and burn down my village to save it. A game-used Gretzky hockey stick seemed like the appropriate spear of destiny, as I was trying to skate to where the puck was *gonna* be.

The day of the screening, a man named Shawn Chaulk took three flights from upper Alberta to Salt Lake City, Utah. The owner of the world's largest collection of game-used and game-worn Wayne Gretzky memorabilia, he was carrying my Excalibur: the last stick Gretzky ever touched as an Edmonton Oiler. Mere months later, the Trade of the Century would send the Great One to Los Angeles, where he'd play for the Kings, and nothing would ever be the same again.

Malcolm had quietly looked for Shawn on the Web, asking him if he could help us out with the off-kilter wish.

Being a Gretzky acolyte like me, Shawn understood my friend's bizarre request to borrow the most significant stick in his collection for one night, so it could lend a fat film-maker some nerve at the Sundance Film Festival. The guy spent the better part of a day on planes to reach us, but it was an assist of which even Wayne himself would be proud, I'm sure. I still love Malcolm for making that happen.

Stick in hand, I gave a barn burner of a speech in which I advocated for art and said the business half of the show-business equation was out of control—particularly marketing spending.

"I never wanted to know jack shit about business," I said at one point. "I'm a fat, masturbating stoner. That's why I got into the movie business: I thought that was where fat, masturbating stoners went. And if somebody had told me at the beginning of my career, 'You're going to have to learn so much about business, finance, amortization, all that shit, monetization,' I would have been like, 'Fuck it. I'm just going to stay home and masturbate. That's too much work, man.'"

Then came the moment of truth: Some folks sat through my passionate plea for art because they were waiting to see me dangle and burn at the imagined auction. That's when I brought Jon Gordon up on stage with me, who opened up the bidding for *Red State*. I quickly bid twenty bucks, Jon "sold" me the flick, and boom—I'd picked my distributor in the room, auction style. I then told all assembled, "Ladies and gentlemen, when I came here seventeen years ago, all I wanted to do was sell my movie. And I can't think of anything fucking worse, seventeen years later, than selling my movie to people who just don't fucking get it."

During the speech, I praised Harvey for what he taught me, referring to the creative film distribution Jon and I were planning for *Red State*, but in my heart I was really thanking Harvey for his last lesson—the one he imparted by trying to postpone our screening and then ignoring the film in favor of game stats in the lobby. This was a man who'd asked me to write that Harvey-defense piece after Peter Biskind's book *Down and Dirty Pictures* told a warts-and-all tale of indie film's rise in which Harvey looked a little less than heroic. I could always be counted on as the "*Harvey rocks!*" mouthpiece, and what I said would be given placement in the media because I was known for being overly candid and disastrously honest. As such, aside from making the View Askew movies there, my side gig at Miramax was also credibility clown.

After the screening, Jon and I found a quiet corner and moment to lick our wounds. "The Harvey Boys, sir . . . ," I lamented. "We were literally stupid enough to call our production company the Harvey Boys. And Harvey doesn't even give a fuck. We're alone."

But we weren't alone, we were just *indie*. We were, in fact, the indie-est game in town at *the* indie film festival that year. Everyone else was trying to sell their flicks to the highest bidder, and there we were—the *Harvey* Boys—announcing we were were gonna handle the flick ourselves—like we'd been taught by our sensei.

Harvey's brother Bob turned out to be the silver lining to the Weinstein cloud. Bob had skipped the debut screening of *Red State* in favor of the Jets game, so he was at the screening in the Park City Library the next morning instead. After the flick, he grabbed me in the hallway and said, "Who knew you could direct action?" It was Bob who gave Jon and me the grown-up props we'd dreamed his brother might've greeted us with the night before. Bob—the genre-junkie brother with his many *Scream* sequels—listened to Jon and me tell him our grand plans for a fifteen-city four-walling tour starting at Radio City Music Hall. Bob's eyes lit up as he anxiously sputtered, "That's how Harvey and I started, back in the old days!" I didn't bother telling him that was our idea: that both Jon and I—the biggest Miramaxateers on the planet, possibly bigger cheerleaders for the dream that was Miramax than even Harvey himself—had based everything we were doing with *Red State* on the nascent days of indie film in Weinstein country. Instead, I just nodded, smiling.

Then Bob inadvertently proved himself more astute and supportive than his brother when (in classic Bob Weinstein fashion) he also gave us his cut suggestions. And even though our flick didn't belong to Miramax, or Dimension, or the Weinstein Company, I took a couple of Bob's notes—for old times' sake.

Some of the bloggers and press who'd come to watch me hold an auction to the highest bidder that they themselves had created were fucking *pissed* that I deked 'em out. The long, sharp knives came out almost immediately after the first screening ended, but that was okay: It was all part of the plan.

After years of letting inferiors insist in print that I was bad at expressing myself, I was done with the critical community and film press. The concept no longer made sense to me: a handful of loudmouth crackpots who make their parasitic living off of self-expressing about someone else's self-expression, telling that person, essentially, that he or she is expressing themselves *wrong*.

How the fuck can self-expression ever even be classified by someone who's not expressing it *themselves*? It's like someone telling you you're dreaming incorrectly. Only someone who doesn't understand art tells an artist their art somehow failed. How the fuck can art fail? Art can't be graded, because it's going to mean something different to everyone. You can't apply a mathematical absolute to art because there is no one formula for self-expression.

And for the privilege of this? I'm expected to show critics, bloggers, and other members of the movie media my film *free of charge*. The audience has to *pay* to weigh in on my art, but the critical crowd? They get a free meal, then get to throw it up in my face, shit in my sink, and head out the door, unscathed.

Nobody likes to be downgraded from a perceived position of authority, but that was exactly what critics had done to me in their reviews: I was downgraded from a good filmmaker to a bad filmmaker. And I wanted to see what would happen if I did the same to *them*.

So after years of being told by many critics that I wasn't very good at my job, I decided to return the favor. And it all started after I read this tweet by @coked_up_Jesus (likely not the one true Christ):

I gotta say that every day I hate film theory & film students & critics more & more. Where is the fun in movies?

I responded, all in tweets, 140 characters at a clip . . .

Sir sometimes, it's important to turn off the chatter. Film fandom's become a nasty bloodsport where cartoonishly rooting for failure gets the hit count up on the ol' brand-new blog. And if a schmuck like me pays you some attention, score! MORE EYES, MEANS MORE ADVERT $.

But when you pull your eye away from the microscope, you can see that shit you're studying so closely is, in reality, tiny as fuck.

You wanna enjoy movies again? Stop reading about them & just go to the movies. It's improved film/movie appreciation immensely for me.

Seriously: so many critics lined-up to pull a sad and embarrassing train on COP OUT like it was Jennifer Jason Leigh in LAST EXIT TO BROOKLYN.

Watching them beat the shit out of it was sad. Like, it's called COP OUT; that sound like a very ambitious title to you? You REALLY wanna shit in the mouth of a flick that so OBVIOUSLY strived for nothing more than laughs? Was it called SCHINDLER'S COP OUT? Writing a nasty review for COP OUT is akin to bullying a retarded kid who was getting a couple chuckles from the normies by singing AFTERNOON DELIGHT.

It was just ridiculous to watch. That was it for me. Realized whole system's upside down: so we let a bunch of people see it for free and they shit all over it? Meanwhile, people who'd REALLY like to see the flick for free are made to pay? Bullshit: from now on, any flick I'm ever involved with, I conduct critics screenings thusly: you wanna see it early to review it? Fine: pay like you would if you saw it next week.

Well, the critical community went more emo about getting criticized for how *they* express *themselves* than I *ever* did when they'd do the same to me. They scorched the earth defending themselves and their life's work in countless hatchet-job articles, simply because I dared to tell them—as they'd told me so many times before—that they *failed* in some way in *their* careers.

This was not merely sour grapes: This was an absolutely essential step for me as an artist. I knew I could never make something as fucked up and fearless as *Red State* if I gave even a quarter ounce of a shit about what critics would have to say about it eventually. I made *Clerks* without ever once thinking about what a critic might say about it, and that was the purest art I ever put my name on. After that flick, though, I started paying attention to the critics. I started believing what I was told by others: that I had to fear and respect the power of the written or televised critical word, as it could make or break the opening of my film. And when you do that, the art's not pure anymore. I love *Chasing Amy*, but it'll always be tainted for me a bit because it exists as a response to criticism: It's the film I made in order to prove to a select group that *Clerks* wasn't a fluke and that (contrary to what they'd written) *Mallrats* wasn't bad.

I didn't want that for *Red State.* Even in scripted form, it was already an experimental film, way outside the box, and far outside my comfort zone. I was already planning on tackling lots of the critically instilled self-doubt I had with regards to my craft, but I figured none of that was going to be possible if I didn't face down the biggest creative fear I've labored under for nearly two decades: critics.

So to make *Red State* in as similar an artistically free space and mind-set as I was in when I made *Clerks*, I removed the critics from my equation altogether by telling them to go fuck themselves—thus ensuring shitty reviews of the film that would mean the most to me since *Clerks*. Gone was the "What will the critics write and say?" mentality I'd had from *Mallrats* forward; I knew *exactly* what they were gonna write and say at this point, after I'd pissed in the Klean Kanteens they received as gift-bag graft from some studio junket they attended. I'd called down the thunder, so my flick was gonna *get* it! Go read the post-Sundance reviews—particularly the bile from the blogger set, who tried to burn down my house within an hour of the first screening's conclusion. You inspire *that* kind of passion in someone by telling people you're going to deviate from the norm. They *want* to see you fail at that point—and it shows in their prose. And that prose lives online forever, as a testimony to what's more important to them: reviewing a film honestly, or stabbing at the filmmaker with their steely knives. Bitches, you just can't kill the beast. Understand the intelligence K-Z has: If you don't like my lyrics you can press fast-forward.

Despite a Chicken Little–like litany of "It's never gonna work" pieces, or charges that I was "imploding," a month and change after Sundance the SModcast Pictures crew took *Red State* on tour across America. It was like a tent revival meeting every night: houses packed with hard-core fans who came to see movie in which a whack job preaches fire and brimstone to a devoted group of followers. And after the credits rolled, *another* whack job would gleefully bound onstage and reveal how all *his* magic tricks were done to a devoted group of followers. The irony was not lost on any of us.

Jon Gordon, Jen Schwalbach, Meghan Quinlan, Alan Wysocki, James Smith (no relation), projectionist Trevor, and I all lived on the bus for the better part of two months, going to sleep in one state and waking up in another—just like the kids in *Almost Famous*. Clovis kept the moving house party safely on the road while Jen would lead wine-fueled sing-alongs well into the night after each show. Making *Red State* had been a liberating exercise in punk rock filmmaking, and being on the *Red State* USA Tour made you feel like you were in an indie rock band, gigging night after night.

At the tour opener in Radio City Music Hall, we made $160,000 from one screening and landed on the list of Top 10 per-theater averages of all time, behind a slew of Disney cartoons. With the exception of Parks (who doesn't like to fly), most of the cast was onstage for the Q&A. John Goodman brought the house down when he channeled a little *Lebowski*, screaming "SHUT THE FUCK UP, DONNY!" to an elated audience member.

In Boston, we started counting the audience's spontaneous applause moments: nine in all. At each screening, I'd sit in the balcony or back row and live tweet my observations and the crowd's reactions, hash-tagged under various, SModified city names, like #SMoston and #SMohio. I'd write about the regional differences and reactions to the violence, making me feel a little like The Architect in *Matrix Revolutions*: "*Interesting: Your predecessors didn't find Goodman's 'giant cross' line as amusing as you. Ergo, they were numbskulls.*"

It was the way releasing a film *could* be, far from the assembly line of spin and hype. Gone were the junkets, gone were the eight-figure marketing campaigns: It was just filmmaker, film, and audience, communing like hippies. I'd gotten very lucky with *Clerks* inasmuch as my first flick was plucked from obscurity and nursed to good health by Harvey and Co., looked out for by scores of caregivers. I didn't have to struggle like most indie filmmakers, and I suffered no loss of livelihood or home trying to make my art. Once Miramax bought *Clerks*, I could call myself an indie filmmaker while enjoying the benefits of a studio filmmaker: I knew that every flick I made would get a theatrical release. But here I was, nearly two decades later, learning to crawl again. Investing all that time and giving up all that money ultimately paid out in the most treasured coin there is: contentment. And for the first time since I made *Clerks*, I truly felt like the indie filmmaker I was so often described as.

But nobody in this business cares about how good *Red State* may have made me *feel*. Film is a commercialized art form, which means there are those who'll always grade what we did on the least interesting, least creative aspect of the medium: what it cost and what it's made. Dollars, not sense. So for those folks, here's a look at the *Red State* spread sheet . . .

Over the course of the fifteen shows of the *Red State* USA Tour, we made almost one million dollars from ticket and merchandise sales. A few times we had the highest per-screen average in the country. We averaged eleven hundred people a night per screening.

The flick cost five million to make but four million after the California tax incentive. Our *Red State* investors were very cool about letting us handle the American theatrical distribution ourselves, providing that their investment would be covered as soon as possible—something very few production entities even offer, let alone deliver on. Invest a million dollars in almost *any* production and you *rarely, if ever*, get your money back within five years, let alone within the year. You take the million we made on the tour, you add that to the two million we pulled in from foreign sales, and you add to *that* two million more from Lionsgate for the VOD and home video rights, and another million from Netflix for the streaming rights, and you'll notice our gains were higher than our spending. And without any dopey marketing figures to have to recoup, simple math dictates *Red State* is in the black.

And for that, I have you, the audience, to thank. Many, many thanks for making me look like the smartest guy in the room.

But none of it would've been possible without a slew of people helping make this whimsy a reality. Jenny Schwalbach, Jon Gordon, Meghan Quinlan, Jeff Hyman, David Dinerstein, our New York financier, our Canadian financiers NVSH— these are the *"Why Not?"* people.

There are plenty of *"Why?"* people in the world. Whenever you hit them with an idea, they start in with their bullshit.

"Why bother?"

"Why try that?"

"Why do you think you're better than everyone else?"

"Why?"

To counteract this, simply surround yourself with folks who ask only "Why *not*?" As in . . .

"Wanna make a movie?"

"Sure. Why *not*?"

Remember: It costs nothing to encourage an artist, and the potential benefits are staggering. A pat on the back to an artist now could one day result in your favorite film, or the cartoon you love to get stoned watching, or the song that saves your life. Discourage an artist, you get absolutely nothing in return, ever. I've spent the better part of my career getting up after movies and encouraging potential artists in the audience to give it a shot, pointing to myself as proof that anybody can make their dreams come true. I don't do this altruistically: I'm selfishly insuring that I have cool shit to watch one day by encouraging *anybody* to follow passions like film or storytelling. I've been sending a message to the next generation of filmmakers for the last two decades: get ready, 'cause you're up next.

As I left the Sundance stage after my post-screening filibuster that night, I bumped into two such future filmsters: a couple of twentysomething dudes in the crowded hallway exit who were telling me how much they dug the flick and the speech, until one of them nearly knocked me dead when he said, with all the earnestness and passion of indie film *incarnate . . .*

"*You can do this.*"

The whole *Red State* Sundance premiere sometimes feels like a dream, but that kid and his imparted sentiment of encouragement? He was about as real as raincoats. That guy was a thinner, better-looking, more-pussy-getting version of me, circa '94. And 1994-me didn't say, "You fucking idiot! Do what everyone else does and sell your flick and spend to open it!" He kinda said, "Skate, bitch . . . ," knowing full well that if I pulled this off, it'd be easier for him to get *his* flicks out there and express *himself.*

That moment meant the world to me; I'll take it to my grave.

Just like the moment I'd later share with Michael Parks and the greatest filmmaker of my generation.

CHAPTER TEN

The Glowing Shit
That Was in the Briefcase:

Red State, Part III

S *lacker* was the movie that changed my life, but it was a film I'd see almost a year later, featuring a diamond heist pulled by Madonna-savvy hoods in black suits that'd have a dramatic impact on *what* I'd write about. Whoever made *that* movie seemed awfully geeky—like *me.*

Back as far as childhood, I'd try to do things just as well as a normie (sometimes even better), but at the end of the day, my gut, thunder thighs, and childbearing hips earmarked me as somehow less than others. But what was a curse in youth became a blessing in adulthood. Being fat meant relying on a sense of humor to keep from getting my ass kicked simply for an inability to stop at *one* Devil Dog. Bugs Bunny never seemed to get beat up, so lots of us fat kids went for the devil-may-care, smartest-rabbit-in-the-room personality. Do that for ten thousand hours across childhood, and when you're in your twenties, if you apply yourself, you can do it for a living. But it all stems from being *different* somehow—and not in a way that's usually celebrated 'til after years of eating shit.

I suspected Quentin Tarantino was a kindred spirit. I'd purchased and read a bootlegged, xeroxed copy of the *Reservoir Dogs* screenplay before even seeing the flick, but as I watched jewel thieves debate the etiquette of tipping in a movie theater that first time in 1992, I *knew* that, like me, Quentin Tarantino had spent lots of time alone in the dark, dreaming about movies. Different dark room, different movies, same dream.

One of my fondest memories of my film career is seeing *Pulp Fiction* before even the 1994 Cannes jury, in a theater packed with Harvey's handpicked tastemakers. The flick was like nothing we'd ever seen before while still being as familiar and comfortable as your favorite jeans (and just as cool). *Pulp* was thrilling, then mesmerizing, then educational: I walked out of that screening and started redrafting *Dogma*. Quentin had not only taken it up a notch, he'd also thrilled me with wild tonal changes throughout the narrative. The flick is a roller coaster of a film: funny, then serious, then fucked-up, then iconic, then quietly beautiful. It's a mind-chigger of a movie that burrows into your cranial hard drive and won't let you forget it. You see that movie, it's a part of you forever.

There were always boatloads of benefits in being part of the Miramax family during the dynasty years—not the least of which was seeing movies first (for free). In 1995, Bob Weinstein invited me to a screening of Dimension's post-*Pulp* Quentin/Robert Rodriguez team-up picture, *From Dusk Till Dawn*. Quentin had already taught me you could talk about anything in movie dialogue (not solely plot), and he'd already taught me you could fuck with the audience and give 'em a bunch of different movies at once, and they won't hate you for it (in fact, they'll love you). Do something *different*—stand apart from the rest—and you'll always have the audience on your side. And even though *Dusk* wasn't expected to be much more than a popcorn flick, I was curious about whether Quentin had anything to teach me *this* time.

Michael Parks *owns* the opening of *Dusk* and just about *any* flick he's in, for that matter. As a fan of performance (I love when actors act), seeing Parks for the first time was akin to discovering masturbation: Where had *this* been all my life? The man delivers dialogue in the least obvious manner and *never* smells like he's acting. After the screening, I told my producer and friend Scott Mosier, "I wanna work with that guy one day. Can you imagine what you'd learn over the course of production, sitting at the feet of an acting Yoda like him?"

It took fifteen years, but *Red State* finally put me onto a set with the actor who is lots of actors' *favorite* actor. And the legend, Parks, had been introduced to me by the legend, Tarantino.

So when I went up to Quentin's house to watch *Red State* with him *and* Parks together, it was akin to going to meeting your girlfriend's ex-boyfriend—the one she's still really good friends with. And while a critic's thoughts on my flicks didn't interest me any longer, hearing the opinion of a guy who directly inspired the movie? The opinion of a Grand Master Filmmaker? I'd be way interested in hearing *that*.

Parks and I met in Quentin's courtyard driveway—where the Pussy Wagon sits idle, forever awaiting The Bride's escape. After introducing Rie Rasmussen, the director of *Human Zoo* who was going to be watching the flick with us, Quentin came clean.

"I've already watched it," he chuckled. "I watched it Friday night. By myself."

At which point everything in me went away but the filmmaker, and I asked that all-important question . . .

"Did you dig it?"

"I fucking loved it! That's why I'm—"

I didn't let him finish. I just hugged him as hard as I could.

You see, Quentin's was the only review that was ever gonna matter. *Red State* was inspired by the man's work, his casting choices, his daring *Pulp Fiction* tonal shifts. With *Red State*, I didn't want to make a Kevin Smith movie. This time, I wanted to make a movie that was Quentin Tarantino by way of the Coen brothers, with just a soupçon of Kev. And to have Quentin not only watch the flick but also dig it enough to watch it again in the span of seventy-two hours? That's graduation day, folks. Ain't no reason for me to continue as a filmmaker past *Hit Somebody*—because I scored the respect of a Grand Master.

He said it stood beside *Chasing Amy* as his favorite of mine, and then said, "Your words coming out of Parks was perfect." He loved that he never knew where it was going. He just plain loved it—which was all that the guy who made the film wanted to hear, considering how often throughout the writing and shooting of *Red State*, he'd wonder, "What would Quentin do?" before executing a shot, making an edit, or even eating lunch on set.

"Well, we really don't have to watch it again now . . . ," I started to say.

"No, I wanna watch it again," he countered. "And I wanna show Rie."

Rie nodded and said, "He's been talking about it all day."

You think *that's* nirvana for any filmmaker—knowing your artistic better is willing to watch your flick *twice* within seventy-two hours? You'll never know true, pure bliss as a filmmaker until you've sat *beside* Quentin watching your own flick.

As we all know, the man *loves* movies. Tarantino is the most interactive audience member on the planet. He makes a home screening feel like a full house at the multiplex. Even in a room of four, he will make you feel like you're screening at the Palais. It's not an act and it's certainly no hustle; he watches movies like he makes them—with pure, unadulterated joy over the concept of storytelling.

This screening had the added bonus, the heightened effect, of having Parks with us there in the room, next to two dudes who love him so much, they were geeking out over every little nuance, eye shift, grumble, and song. *This* is the only person in the world who'd ever appreciate Michael's performance on the same level I do. As he watched Parks act, Quentin communicated *exactly* what I felt every day we shot and feel every time I watch *Red State*: Michael Parks is the single greatest living actor on the planet, and he should be working *lots* more.

After the credits, we talked about how weird it was that Harvey didn't make *Red State*, as it's clearly a Miramaxian flick, intended to invoke the golden age of the mini-major, right down to the design of the Harvey Boys logo, which aped the classic Miramax Films logo of the mid-'90s. Quentin offered some soothing insight into the Weinstein *Red State* pass-over, as even *he'd* felt the confusing sting of the brothers doing a blank face when they twice passed on *Hostel*—a flick with Quentin's name on it. Miramax was often called "the house that Quentin built" by Harvey himself. If Harvey and Bob could pass on the guy who built their house, they could certainly say no to the mooch smoking dope with his friends in the back pool house.

Quentin compared our self-distribution experiment to an old grindhouse release, at which point I told him *why* it felt so familiar to him: Back in 1997, he'd actually suggested it himself, during a South by Southwest panel featuring an indie dream team: Linklater, Tarantino, Rodriguez, Steven Soderbergh, Mike Judge, and me.

Someone asked a question about how to secure theatrical distribution. Quentin asked the audience how many people in the room wanted to make films and how many were potential distributors-in-training. There wasn't a hand up for distributor. Quentin said that the next generation of filmmakers should distinguish themselves by forming distribution companies instead of production companies . . . and that always stuck with me. I kept waiting for it to happen. But that ol' indie spirit, it don't wait forever. Sooner or later, indie spirit rolls up the sleeves and says, " 'Scool—we'll just do it *ourselves*." And *Red State* is *very* indie.

We eventually made our way into the living room,

where the world's biggest movie fan then did something that touched me more than his praise for my flick: He produced a videocassette.

In Quentin's house, this is a wholly remarkable feat unto itself based on the amount of stuff he's got piled up: old movie posters, DVDs, laser discs, VHS tapes, lunch boxes, juke-boxes, toys, artwork, and film prints. He lives like Arthur (the Dudley Moore version). The videocassette he pulled out was nothing short of magical, a relic from an old world and the seed of what was to come for him, and then later, even *me*.

"This is my 'Best of Michael Parks' tape. See?" He held out the decades-old VHS cassette that still bore a faded label delineating it as such. "I made it back in the eighties, after I saw him in this amazing TV movie called *Club Life*. Well, the movie's not amazing, but Michael is—so I taped his best scenes. A few years later, he did the best work of his career in *The China Lake Murders*, and I've got scenes from that and *Spiker*, where he plays a soccer coach."

"Volleyball," Michael added, rolling a cigarette.

You consider yourself a movie geek until you talk movies with Quentin. He's very much like Jason Mewes, inasmuch as he'll find the good in *anything*. As he played his favorite scenes, I remembered using my dad's tape recorder to snag the audio from *Jaws* when it finally ran on ABC (long before the days of cable or home video). This was a kindred spirit: the dude who made a mix tape of one of his favorite actors' best moments in movies nobody—not even the filmmakers themselves—likely remember. You start to see the beauty hidden within the cheese. Nothing about even an '80s exploitation TV movie is dismissed without fair, comprehensive, and artistic consideration.

And all the while, good ol' Michael was like the guest star in a married couple's threesome: All praise, attention, and cock-suckery were bestowed upon him by a pair of filmmakers (one great, one trying) who absolutely adore him. Scene after scene on that tape, it didn't matter what the caliber of the flick on display was considered to be, Parks dropped science. I'll never forget watching Michael watch himself on Quentin's big TV—seeing his life flash before his eyes without that pesky bother of having to draw a final breath. In a time when no one cared a tin whistle for an acting talent as staggering as Michael's, Quentin didn't carry merely a torch for Michael Parks, he carried the entire Chicago Fire. Because of that, I got to make the best film I've ever made.

As a filmmaker and an artist, Quentin has always been, for lack of a better expression, a role model. He showed me it was okay to write dialogue about pop culture, which allowed me to write movie dialogue about *other* movie dialogue—the language of my cine-centric world. He showed me it was okay to let characters ramble and pontificate. He showed me it was okay to mix comedy and jaw-dropping, scene-stopping violence in a movie. He showed me Michael Parks. I made *Red State* hoping it would be as cool as a Quentin Tarantino film, never dreaming I'd get to watch it *with* him. And as I was leaving Quentin's that night, I gave him a hug and said, "I'm so glad you dig it." Quentin quickly shot back, "I fucking *love* this movie, okay?"

Red State would go on to win Best Film and Michael Parks would win Best Actor at the Sitges Film Festival in Spain, the world's biggest genre festival. But as sweet as that was, nothing else that ever happens to *Red State* will ever be as satisfying as the moment when the guy who inspired the movie said he fucking loved the movie.

As the Year in *Red* ended, I received a package from Shawn Chaulk—the Albertan who brought a hockey stick all the way to Sundance for me to hold onstage. Inside, I found a photo of an Oilers-era Wayne Gretzky, *signed by the Great One himself!* And while it probably won't qualify as an actual "*fresh*" movie critique at RottenTomatoes.com, it's a review of *Red State* that shoots *and* scores.

"Dear Kevin—*Red State* rocks!"

And with that, the puck caught up.

CHAPTER ELEVEN

Talking Shit

After *Hit Somebody*, I'm going to retire from directing. Everything else I'm working on will continue as-is or hopefully grow, but I know it's time to fold up the director's chair.

I've been incredibly blessed the past two decades. Back in 1991, I got this idea in my head that I wanted to be a filmmaker, even though I'd never shown interest in film study or craft. Less than three years later, my first flick got picked up by the biggest distributor on the block. For over a decade following, I got to make every film I ever wanted. I even got to make a movie for a bona fide "original six" Hollywood studio. It's been twenty years of wonder and win. But it *has* been twenty years. Two decades. Ten films.

I'm not done yet, but I've been feeling it since *Zack and Miri Make a Porno*: What I was once zealously passionate about has simply become my job. I didn't burn or yearn to make films like I did in the early days; movies became just what I did for a living. I'd made one incredibly uncharacteristic and bold move that resulted in an entire career and then reaped the benefits for years, keeping my head up, stick down, grinding out a body of work. I could certainly execute . . . but I'd stopped elevating. And while I'm grateful for all that I've been given or allowed to do in film, that means it's time to go. And after the next flick, go I shall.

Even Wayne Gretzky hung up the skates. He could've gone another season, but after playing for twenty years, as much as he loved the game that gave him everything, he said good-bye. In his heart and head (and probably in his muscles and joints), Gretzky knew he couldn't do what he used to anymore.

It's tough realizing you're done doing that which *defined* you—in my case, since the early '90s. And it's *frightening*. You're torn between not wanting to overstay your welcome and just doing the job to keep the status quo; you're haunted by the thought, "What on earth will I do with the rest of my life?"

Point being: There's an accepted norm, and when you deviate from it, life gets more difficult. Swimming against the mainstream is exhausting, and you often look at all the other kids in motorboats, wondering why the fuck you can't simply toe the line like everyone else. As much as you want to walk your own path, you're terrified of standing apart because the pack offers security, normalcy, convenience, protection, and identity.

So here's the tough shit: Security, normalcy, convenience, protection, and identity are opiates you've gotta wean yourself off before you can be an *individual.* You can't stand out if you're blending in.

When I first told my friends Bryan and Walt that I wanted to be a director, over a pizza in Highlands, circa 1991—that I was going to enroll in the Vancouver Film School, learn a thing or two, then bring that knowledge home so we could all make a movie—their reaction made it seem I'd actually just informed them I was slipping under the table so they could sword-fight in my mouth. And while my parents didn't share that specific reaction, they, too, were taken aback.

"Not a lot of people ever make it in that business," I was told. "You've gotta be really good to get through the door."

But that smelled like horseshit. I'd been watching movies for two decades at that point and had seen enough average, mundane, or crap flicks to know that I had as good a shot as any of the folks who'd made them. Sure, I'd never be Martin Scorsese, but maybe one day, if I worked at my craft constantly and played the game with pure passion and will over skill . . .

Maybe, instead, I could be Kevin Smith.

Two decades later, I'm still no Scorsese. Instead, I'm *me.* And while I don't have the eye, talent, sense, or height of Scorsese, I'm still *called* a director—just like Scorsese. But Scorsese will likely leave this world toes-up off a movie set. He's the gen-u-ine article: a bona fide, natural-born film-maker. Me? I'll likely leave this world on a McDonald's floor, after eating one too many McGriddles. So before that happens, I'm gonna wrap up my directing career and go explore the *rest* of the art forms—y'know, the *less expensive* ones.

Self-expression is the heart of all arts—even movies. But

unlike the rest of the arts, movies are a costly fashion in which to tell the world what you're feeling. If I could paint, I'd slap some color on a canvas and it'd communicate who I am. If I could sing, I'd open my mouth in song and you'd know what I was trying to say. But I'm a filmmaker—which means I'm the artist who says, "I need to express myself! Quick, get me twenty million dollars and Ben Affleck!"

But with the advent of technology comes new art forms, most of which offer far less costly ways to express myself—both in dollars and common sense. My first language isn't cinema, it's English. And my true strength is not in assembling pictures that tell a story; it's *talking* a blue streak. I can talk for hours and all it costs me is time, not dimes. And even better? When you listen to my stories via spoken word, *you're* doing all the heavy lifting *for* me. I don't have to string together visuals or move a camera; it's theater of the mind, so the listener builds word pictures for me in their head, directing their own internal movie based on the yarn I'm spinning.

Still, even given that I've found other ways to tell you stories that make more sense, it was tough deciding to leave directing behind, as it's all I've been doing for nearly twenty years now. But I didn't make *Clerks* because I wanted to be in the movie business; I made *Clerks* because I wanted to be a filmmaker. I wanted to tell stories, and doing it cinematically made the most sense at the time—that time being 1994. But making films opened lots of interesting doors and afforded me the opportunity to play in multiple artistic sandboxes—so by 2007, the toys in the other yard were starting to look (and *be*) a lot more fun. And in a world where Dad died screaming, I'm not going to go out with any regrets.

So I quietly accepted the fact that, for the second time in my life, I was going to tell people something extremely uncharacteristic: Twenty years ago, it was "I want to be a filmmaker." Twenty years later, it's now "I want to be an artist."

Some artists suffer alone, but I've always tried to involve my friends and family in my art as well. This isn't altruistic at all: If you're surrounded by people you like and admire, you never feel like you're actually working; it's more like hanging out with a purpose. Hire your friends if you can, but understand it means, one day, you may have to fire a friend as well. So if you choose your friendployees carefully, even if you're paying their salaries, they're not working *for* you—they're working *with* you.

If we are the sum total of all our experiences, then who I am today has everything to do with who I was back in the day. And back in the day, all I did was hang out with Bryan Johnson and Walt Flanagan. My life will always boil down to two eras: B.C. and A.D. B.C. stands for, of course, "Before *Clerks*"—when I was just a fat guy, not the Fat Guy Who Made *Clerks*. A.D. stands for "After Dante"—the existence I've led since Miramax bought my first flick back in 1994. Bryan and Walt have always been the bridge between those two eras.

Walt Flanagan was my reluctant guru. Circa 1989, we worked together at the Highlands Recreation Center for a year, during which time he'd loan me copies of *The Dark Knight Returns*, *Watchmen*, and *Mage*. The broad strokes you know about me—"Kev likes comics and hockey!"—have everything to do with Walter. He fuel-injected those passions into my heart because they were *his* passions. Whenever he spoke about comics with such wonder and awe, he came

across with all the fire and conviction of a fundamentalist preacher. It was Walt's interest in comics that sparked
mine.

That era was an age of wonders. We'd spend weekends
going to comic book shows in New York City, cherry-
picking from the wall books and discount boxes 'til dusk—at
which point we'd scamper back home to the Monmouth
County suburbs, where nobody's ever been mugged. When
there wasn't a weekend show to hit, we'd drive from one
end of Jersey to the other with a phone book, tracking down
hole-in-the-wall hobby shops, hoping to find still-racked
first printings of Alan Moore's *Batman: The Killing Joke.*

During those many hours on toll roads, we'd talk about
the story arcs and specific issues we loved, and—like all
comic fans—how we would've improved plot points or dialogue with our fan-boy attention to detail and love of conti-
nuity.

"Wouldn't it be awesome to work for DC Comics?"
I'd ask. And even Walt Flanagan—who was never really a
dreamer so much as a doubting-Thomas pragmatist—would
say, "Yeah . . ."

Unlike Walt, Bryan Johnson *was* a dreamer. I started
hanging out with Bry more and more when Walt began
dating Debby Grasso (whom he'd marry a few years later).
Bryan and I tried to attend Brookdale Community College
together a few times in the early '90s, but it never really
worked out because we *were* Dante and Randal: overedu-
cated and seriously fucking lazy outsiders who didn't drink,
smoke, or do drugs. Our post–high school routine went
something like this: We'd try a little college until we realized

it wasn't for us, then quit and hurl ourselves back into the job market.

And *market* was the key word, as I was the king of the convenience store circuit. From Highlands to Atlantic Highlands to Leonardo, it was all counter terrorism for me and Big Bry. Convenience stores were easy and never really felt like work, primarily because it never *was* work whenever Bryan Johnson was around. We took loads of shit from friends and the occasional customer who insisted we were wasting our lives behind a register, but we loved Quick Stop. We met interesting people there, as well as mouthy assholes, the desperate and the damned. We learned life's beautiful and universal truths while slinging cigarettes, skin mags, and Entenmann's cakes. We were shaped by the people we waited on, trained by quick-witted battles against fourteen-year-old would-be shoplifters. And most important, we got to eat all the snacks and drink all the chocolate milk we wanted, *all day long.* That's a *big* bucket of win.

But what would eventually happen is Bry and I would start to panic that the rest of our lives were fucked because we didn't get college degrees. All our high school betters were working toward their bachelors at universities, and we couldn't even get it together enough to get associate degrees at a local CC. So we'd psych each other up to be like everyone else, head back to Brookdale, and enroll in a new round of courses that never exactly indicated our eventual directions in life.

Classes sucked, but Bry and I would entertain each other with cartoons and poems about our classmates. One of my favorite pastimes at Brookdale was to see how hard I could laugh without being noticed or caught in class, during lectures. I'd never had a funnier wingman with whom I could sharpen my comedic teeth, and all that practice would eventually lead to a career in entertainment.

Bry and Walt had no idea they were arming their friend for a life of paid play in movies, but they never could've imagined that our long hours of conversation and analysis we'd devote to the mundane and seemingly unimportant would aggregate into an empire decades later—and that they were, in essence, investing in their own futures. All that chatter, all those conversations, and all those laughs would be the fossil fuel that eventually powered one very large podcasting concern.

And ironically, that podcasting concern would be born out of *actual* concern: concern for the health and well-being of another powerful, life-changing friendship.

I met Scott Mosier in 1992 on our first day at the Vancouver Film School. At first glance, I was sure I hated him: He was a leather-jacket-wearing, dual-citizenship-carrying pretty boy who likely never had to beg for a handy. Within the first two weeks of school, we were thrown together for a class exercise that eventually forced us into conversation. Thankfully, I'd been training with conversational ninjas in the delicate art of what-if scenarios for the previous five years, so I was able to free-associate about our instructors, movies, and pop culture, and all of it was biting, sharp, and funny. The Bry and Walt influence in New Jersey had led to film school coffee-shop conversations and dissections of pop culture in the True North with Scott, a world away in Vancouver, British Columbia, which would lead to *Clerks* and everything after.

But a decade or so after we burst onto the scene with *Clerks*, all Mos and I ever did together was work. Sure, we'd crack wise and bullshit through commentary tracks of our flicks whenever we put the laser discs or DVDs together, but long gone were the awesome hours of musing about nothing while trying to make each other laugh. We'd become boring ol' grown-ups, ever entrenched in conversations about work.

I suggested to Scott that we sit down once a week to record one of those podcasts I'd started hearing about on the Internet. It sounded like homegrown radio and was described to me in myriad ways before I understood it was my future.

"These podcasts are like doing a commentary track without a movie," I told Mos.

The idea was to record once a week and then post the conversations online. The public availability of the show was an integral part of the equation because it encouraged accountability from lazy motherfuckers; if we knew an audience was going to be listening, there was a much better chance we'd make an effort to sit down and record every week, thus improving the overall health and fun of our friendship. Otherwise, it'd decline into catch-as-catch-can non-existence, ultimately taking a backseat to almost anything else in our lives, thus defeating the purpose of its creation.

So on February 5, 2007, Scott and I sat down to record the very first *SModcast*—the name a rudimentary combination of *S* for *Smith* and *M* for *Mosier*, spliced with the word *podcast*. The format was simple: dopey free-associative conversations that sounded like the same ones you have with your friends. We kept a fairly regular weekly schedule, taking weeks off only when we went into production. The show was out there years before the great pod rush, so we were able to build up a dedicated following: First, five thousand weekly listeners, then twenty thousand, then one hundred thousand, two hundred thousand, three hundred thousand.

Part of the appeal of the show became the periodic tastes of the East Coast flavor. Whenever I was back in Jersey without Scott, I'd have Bry and Walt join me as guests on *SModcast*. Their shows always received huge feedback, so I started encouraging them to record their own weekly podcast. But while those guys are both true originals, they're both shit at self-starting as well. Neither Bry nor Walt are cursed with the amount of unreasonable self-esteem that's required to initiate something outside the box—that reasonable amount of unreasonability.

But I always knew they had it buried somewhere deep within them because we all grew up in New Jersey, you see—the state that resides squarely in the shadow of its far sexier sister, New York. Jersey was the butt of toxic-waste jokes—the armpit state. It wasn't a destination, it was a conduit to Philly or the shit hole you visited only when you wanted to watch Giants games and maybe play the slots. The state least likely to amount to much. Dismissed as inferior, folks from Jersey tend to try harder. We know we've got a perceived deficit, and in the same way that a fat man eats pussy, we overproduce to make up for it. Jersey makes you cum twice *before* it even pulls its dick out. We have to; we're New Jersey.

Bryan says he had one foot on a chair and a noose

around his neck when he finally recorded the first episode of *Tell 'Em, Steve-Dave*—the award-winning weekly podcast he records back in Jersey with Walt and Brian Quinn. Named for a line from *Mallrats* that Walt says to Bry, the show was something of a medical marvel: It was the talking cure for Bry's blues. Each week, he'd spill his head out to Dr. Flanagan—whose no-nonsense, tough-love approach to therapy makes Dr. Phil look like Dr. Seuss. And each week, the feedback was incredible. The audience built rapidly and Bryan could no longer deny that his thoughts and opinions—his *life*—mattered.

It didn't take long to transition *Tell 'Em* to a live show, and suddenly, two guys who never expressed interest in being on a stage were free-associating and conversing in the same way I always loved listening to back at the Highlands Recreation Center, but doing it in front of hundreds of appreciative people who were paying money to see them talk. But the best magic trick was yet to come.

Elyse Seiden wasn't just an executive producer on *Red State*, she was really the lynchpin of the flick. Elyse was the first person to find actual money to make *Red State*, and when we were in postproduction, she asked if I'd meet with her friend Charlie Corwin, who ran a small production company called Original Media. At our meeting, Charlie asked if I had any geeky ideas for AMC—the home of the best television on television right now: *Mad Men, Breaking Bad, The Walking Dead*. He said AMC was looking for a show that the *Dead* audience might also enjoy, and Charlie thought I might have an idea. I said a comic book store reality show would be fun for that audience, not to mention inexpensive to produce. You could scour America for the most erudite, colorful comic shop cast you could find, and after rolling cameras for two months there'd be an entire season of episodes. Charlie said he'd take it back to AMC.

A few days later, Charlie said AMC responded well to the notion. The next step would be shooting a pilot presentation. In an effort to keep the cost down, I suggested using my comic book store in Red Bank, New Jersey—Jay and Silent Bob's Secret Stash.

"The guys that work there will be fine for the presentation," I told Charlie. "If you wanna hear what they sound like, spin a few episodes of *Tell 'Em, Steve-Dave*."

The next week, Charlie called back and said, "We don't have to scour the earth. These guys *are* the show."

Elyse and Charlie brought the AMC execs down to Red Bank to meet Bry and Walt, and suddenly, we were shooting an AMC-financed pilot at my comic book store, starring two of my best friends in the world—solely because their podcast was funny and interesting. Bry didn't merely talk himself off a ledge; he talked himself into a TV show called *Comic Book Men*. On AMC, no less—the 1984 Edmonton Oilers of cable! The mid-'90s Miramax of current-day television! *Tell 'Em, Steve-Dave* turned out to be a hysterical fountain of eternal youth, but it also saved Bryan Johnson's life.

Meanwhile, on the other side of the country, the talking cure was saving the life of another Jersey best friend as well—a best friend who was also the sharpest tool in my garage-band world, gifted to me decades past by those twin suns Bry and Walt, the great givers of life.

There are likely more pictures of me standing next to Jason Mewes in existence than there are pictures of me standing next to either my wife or child. That's because

Mewes has always been *both* to me: wife *and* child. As Jay and Silent Bob, we've been professionally married for years; privately, he's been the son I never had or wanted.

About two years ago, Jason Mewes was on a one-way trip to Shitsville, courtesy of his old Lex Luthor: drugs. Sure, Mewes had danced with Mr. Brownstone and friends before and come out the victor—but that was when he was single. It's much easier to fuck up your own life and try to rebuild than it is to fuck up your *wife's* life and hope she's still around so you can tell her you're sorry once you've spanked the monkey off your back again.

As human beings, we govern our actions with our deepest fears. But if you name that shit, you claim that shit: Let enough people into your closet and you'll find there's no more room for skeletons. Leave yourself nowhere to hide and you can live life unguarded.

For years, I'd been telling Mewes, "You have to start talking about the drugs, sir. Tell the stories, warts and all." But as fearless as Jay normally was in his approach to life, he was terrified to confess he'd used needles. "I'll never get another job if I tell people I've shot heroin," he'd say. I'd list actors who'd junked out and come back from their addiction, but Jason was resolute: The public discussion of his private shames was all acceptable fun and games—*except* when it came to heroin.

Ironically, it was telling people all the dirty details of doing dope that finally set Jason Mewes free. In the fall of 2010, roughly six months after the start of *Tell 'Em, Steve-Dave*, Mewes and I started recording a podcast called *Jay and Silent Bob Get Old*, appropriating the names of the characters that made us famous and using them as an umbrella under which Jay could tell *his* stories and lay out his troubled (albeit hysterical) past every week in what's basically a weekly intervention, or one of Bill W.'s *meetings*, if you will: Every Wednesday, you get to see or hear Jason save his own life. You'd be shocked by how inspiring it is to watch a man battle substance abuse with the only weapons he's got left: his sense of humor and his lack of self-consciousness.

The beauty of conversation is that you don't need talent or a set of special performance skills to engage in one: *Anybody* can hold a convo. I started to wonder: If I had a really interesting or funny conversation with my friends and we relocated that conversation to a proscenium, would an audience pay just to watch us speak?

Even though Scott is not a stage-oriented, limelight-seeking kinda cat like me, two years after we started *SModcast*, I got him to do the show live up on a stage for charity, in front of over a thousand people at the Sanderson Centre in Brantford, Ontario, the hometown of Wayne Gretzky, during Walter Gretzky's annual street hockey tournament. In front of a sold-out house, quite like Frampton, Mosier came alive. Fueled by the appreciative crowd, Mos crushed onstage, leaping nimbly from topic to topic, slinging jokes and voices, bringing the house down. A few months later, we did another live show, this time at the Two River Theater in Red Bank, New Jersey, to help promote *Shootin' the Shit with Kevin Smith* — a book of transcribed episodes of *SModcast*. Attendance was good but not great, so after the show, there was little talk of ever doing *SModcast* live again.

The economic downturn would prove to be my good

fortune, however. Months later, Scott was between jobs and in need of some income. I told him an easy way to make ten or twenty grand would be to tour *SModcast* across the country at little indie rock and comedy clubs. We'd had enough practice talking to each other in a room alone; transitioning that to a stage seemed the next logical step. Mos said yes, so I rented a bus, and we hit the road on April 26, 2010, for the sold-out *Live Nude SMod* tour: York, Pennsylvania; Cleveland, Ohio; Duluth, Minnesota; Fargo, North Dakota; Billings, Montana; and San Francisco, California. A month later, we rented another bus and sold out shows in Philadelphia, Pennsylvania; Columbus, Ohio; and Madison, Wisconsin.

When I got home from the second tour in June, I was musing on Twitter about how much I loved doing *SModcast* live and wished we could do it more often. I tweeted a dream of a black-box theater in Los Angeles, where we could do live podcasts whenever we wanted. My friend Matt Cohen picked up that ball and *ran* with it! He was a creature of improv classes and a student of live comedy, so the idea of a performance space where we could put on our own shows sent the normally sedate stoner slacker into passionate overdrive, and within a day, he found the perfect location on Santa Monica Boulevard: a forty-four-seat black-box theater.

Matt and I partnered up and opened the portcullis on SModcastle—the world's first and only podcast theater—on July 25, 2010. The sold-out prima nocta event featured *SModcast 3D*; *Highlands: A Peephole History*; *Tell 'Em, Steve-Dave*; and *Having Sex, with Katie Morgan*. I can't speak for anyone else, but I felt like I was in *The Little Rascals*, mounting miniature epics in our parents' backyards.

SModcastle gave birth to *Blow Hard*, *SMovieMakers*, *Red State of the Union Q&A*, *Crimson Mystical Mages*, *Starfucking*, *SMarriage*, and more—all the children of the atom that are the SModcast Network.

But while SModcastle was born of *SModcast*, it quickly became the house that *Babble* built, as well as the Meweseum of unnatural history.

After our family moved to Los Angeles permanently in 2002, I became a semiregular visitor to the *Kevin and Bean* morning show on the World Famous KROQ. The highlight for me was always "Showbiz Beat"—"walked" on the airwaves by actor/comic Ralph Garman. Not only did Ralph love geek news, he could also do amazing impressions of folks like TV Batman Adam West—which would then *really* bring the geek news to life. "Showbiz Beat" is a five-minute segment, but whenever I was in the studio with Ralph, it would go ten minutes or more—because as much as we love showbiz, we love to make fun of it and deconstruct it as well. Forget what you've heard about baseball; making fun of your betters is the *real* American pastime.

After years of sitting in on "Showbiz Beat," Ralph suggested we hit up KROQ about doing a Saturday morning show of sorts that'd be like an hour of entertainment news. We recorded a pilot, presented it, and were told nobody wants to hear people talk on the radio anymore—which was cool by me, as I was talking up a storm on the Internet. The Internet was where lots of folks thought talk radio, spoken comedy, and nonpolitical chitchat went to die; in reality, it's where they went to *live*. Podcasting gave on-air talkers one more platform. And unlike radio, users could *choose* what they wanted to listen to at any given moment. And the

Internet got *very* portable over the past ten years—meaning you can carry around thousands of hours of podcasting from *SModcast* in your back pocket and listen whenever you've got time or the notion: while driving, while working, while cleaning the house, while at the gym.

That's because, like your parents or your wife, a podcast doesn't have to be looked at to be listened to. And like a Fleshlight, a podcast is there when *you* need it. Since it's loads of chatter, it's what they call white noise in the background of your day. It's like listening to music but usually much funnier. Since it's audio only, it doesn't have to be stared at to be enjoyed, and it travels well on any MP3 player—which means podcasts can accompany you during your commute. Imagine getting all that mind-blowing free aural, those thick, hot loads of words splashed across your ears, chest, and neck . . . all while accomplishing something *else*. Something more *important*. You're getting shit done when you can kill two birds with one stone, so listening to podcasts actually increases your productivity.

Ralph had never podcasted before, but he'd been in radio for over a dozen years, and radio and podcasting are kinda like Vulcans and Romulans: close enough. After SModcastle opened, Ralph e-mailed me asking, "Wanna do that movie biz show as a podcast instead? We can record it live at your SModcastle." I suggested we call it *Hollywood Babble-On*, and suddenly Ralph and I were off and running.

Since Ralph is on the radio in Los Angeles every morning, he's got his own audience—and *boy*, did that audience turn out for our *Babble*. From the show's debut on, Ralph Garman's fan base (the Garmy) would buy up every one of the forty-four available seats, selling out every week—a feat matched only by Jason Mewes when we launched *Jay and Silent Bob Get Old* a few weeks later.

After months of *Babble-On* and *Get Old* easily selling out our tiny SModitorium, it was clear both shows would flourish in a bigger space. Scott and I had done *SModcast* at comedy clubs a few times, including twice at the world-renowned Improv on Melrose in Los Angeles. So even though SModcastle owner Kev Smith was over the moon about the consistently sold-out shows, costar Kev Smith knew we could easily fill *more* seats. I asked Ralph to sniff around town and see if another club wanted to host *Babble*, and on November 26, 2010, we hit the Jon Lovitz Comedy Club stage running, adding an element that'll make any comedy funnier: *booze!* A few weeks later, *Get Old* moved up to the Lovitz as well—ironically setting an intervention podcast in a bar. Within a few months, SModCo bought the top floor of the Universal CityWalk hot spot, and Jon Lovitz changed the name of his club to the Jon Lovitz Podcast Theatre. SModcastle dropped her drawbridge and moved on up, to a deluxe apartment in the sky, where Ralph and I babble-the-fuck on every Saturday night.

Turns out truth and candor were the gateways to sobriety and success for Jason. Six months after the first episode, I was standing on a stage beside Mewes at the Hard Rock Live in Orlando, where fifteen hundred people had paid to see us talk to each other—partly because they wanted to help him stay clean by hearing him out, and mostly because he's a funny fucker. In less than a year, *Jay and Silent Bob Get Old* begat sold-out live tours here *and* abroad, selling out shows in London, Sydney, Toronto. The guy who didn't want to tell anyone he'd used needles now tells the world funny-as-fuck cautionary tales of his wasted, wastoid youth on a weekly basis and always manages to do it with big laughs and bigger insight.

With all the talking we were doing, it was clear this was all becoming much SMore than just a hobby. So Mewes, Jen, and I tapped his wife, Jordan, to run SModCo, the umbrella company under which we'd podcast, broadcast, tour, shoot, publish, merchandise—a sort of View Askew Part 2. I had the find of the decade on *Cop Out*, when production manager Ray Quinlan told his daughter Meghan to drive me home from the office one night. Meghan quickly became my left hand (not my right, as that is my jerk-off hand, and I can still do that myself, thank you very much), so much so that she came back to California with us after the New York shoot wrapped. She's now the producer of our *SModCo SMorning Show*, as well as the tour manager who put together the *Red State* USA Tour with Jeff Hyman, our show booker at Degy Entertainment. She brought in her fiancé, Alan, who now heads up our SMerchandise division. Together, we built a new clubhouse, where all we do is talk for a living. It's pretty punk rock—dare I say, even a bit *indie*.

Live podcasts are the spine of everything I do now. Live podcasts begat the *Red State* USA Tour and birthed a streaming online radio station dubbed S.I.R.—SModcast Internet Radio—where every morning I host a show with my real wife, Jen, or my man-wife, Jay. And live podcasts led to a TV show: AMC recently announced they'd debut the *Tell 'Em, Steve-Dave*–inspired *Comic Book Men* on February 12, 2012, with *The Walking Dead* as its lead-in—a veritable geek orgy. I'm going to be able to watch Bry and Walt on television once a week, on the best network in the business.

I never would've done any of that shit if it weren't for my friends. Not only did they give me someone to talk to, they gave me interesting things to talk *about*. They even gave me a way to make a living, simply by unwittingly training me with hours of what many deemed useless conversation about nothing very important. Turns out that stuff was the fundamental building blocks of what ultimately became *Clerks* and *SModcast*.

But your friends won't always be there for you: They've got lives of their own. Sometimes, no one will be there for you—because some shit in life you've gotta go through all by yourself. And if you can make it through the tough shit by yourself, you will soar with the eagles . . .

Depending on whether you're too fat to fly . . .

CHAPTER TWELVE

The Shit That Happened on the Plane

When I stepped in the worst, toughest shit of my life, it was because I'd spent the day trying to orally please a bunch of heavy-duty cock-suckers in San Francisco.

Let me back up a second.

My friend Malcolm Ingram is a bear. Not the kind whose porridge you scarf before you take over his comfy bed. No, Malcolm is a proud, albeit large, member of the gay community. Within the gay community, there are many distinctions and subgroups: gay men, lesbian women, transgender people, bisexuals, muscle queens, twinks, and so forth. Malcolm is classified as a bear—that is to say, he's a gay man who's fat and hairy like me, yet has sex with thinner, generally better-looking men. In much the same way my wife is a chubby-chaser—thus explaining how a hideous fucking CHUD such as myself can get some pussy as fine as

Jen Schwalbach's—Malcolm found for himself a community of chubby-chasing *dudes.*

And if these dudes were chicks, they'd be *way* the fuck out of what would be considered Malcolm's league. Hell, even as *dudes*, they're out of his league. Malcolm's fucking *up*—and not in the usual bad way: No matter where he goes in the world, he's always got a good-looking, thin dude hovering around him. I remember the day Malcolm introduced me to one of his first steady boyfriends and the guy was so hot, even *I'd* have thought about temporarily relocating his wiener to my mouth if he said the right thing. He would've looked at home on the cover of *Men's Health*, but here he was, on the arm (and behind closed doors, on the knob) of my best friend from the True North. I was proud of Malcolm: Not only was he boldly punching above his weight class, he was winning title bouts! My bear friend was surrounded by happy, hefty-hungry *cubs*—the nickname given to the guys who're into bears. Isn't that *adorable*?

Back in February 2010, I was scheduled to be in the Bay Area for the Macworld conference. Malcolm revealed he was also in San Francisco that week, but not for Macworld. Malcolm was flying in for the International Bear Rendezvous just across town—a sort of Macworld for big, gay dudes and the shapely men who love (or at least lust for) them.

Malcolm began his pitch. "You're an icon in the bear world, dude. You're like the Angelina Jolie of the bear community. So you should come to IBR with me and do a live podcast while you're already in town for Macworld."

I agreed and started promoting the IBR live podcast on Twitter . . . until Malcolm pulled a Malcolm and started bickering with me about details of the event. Turned off by the unwieldy chip on his shoulder, I bowed out a week before the show. My new plan, instead, was to fly up to the Bay Area with Jen from the Burbank airport, land in Oakland, do the Macworld Q & A, spend the night at the W Hotel trying to have sex with my wife, eat some room service, and come home the next morning.

But after all the drama between me and Malcolm, Jen bailed on the trip altogether. "Just go do Macworld and come home," she said insistently.

I flew to the Oakland airport from Burbank, checked in at the San Francisco W Hotel, walked a block and change to the Moscone Center, and did a Q & A at Macworld. Afterward, a very contrite Malcolm appeared backstage. I had a few hours 'til my flight home, so we hung out, smoked some weed, and buried the hatchet—which sounds erotically charged but merely means we squashed the petty shit from days before. Once we were cool again, naturally Malcolm asked, "So . . . you wanna do the live podcast at IBR still?"

"Sir . . ." I sighed, about to remind him how he'd made his bed and now had to lie in it.

"You wanna do this," Malcolm said seriously. "This may be the only room in the world where you will be sexualized by the entire crowd. You're gonna be talking, and they're all gonna be thinking, 'I'd fuck him.' How can you pass that up—knowing what it feels like to have a whole room full of people lusting after you?"

I corrected him. "*Dudes*, Malcolm . . . a whole room full of *dudes* will be lusting after me."

"What happened to the adventurous Kevin Smith?" he

needled. "Where's the Kevin Smith who made *Clerks*? The ballsy Kevin Smith who took chances? Do it for the experience!"

Jedi mind-tricked by the Carl Lazlo, Esquire of bears, I agreed to rejoin Malcolm for the podcast the next day. Regardless, I still had to fly home that night, as Jen and Harley were expecting me for dinner. I'd fly *back* to the Bay Area the day after and do the live podcast with Malcolm at the International Bear Rendezvous.

When I got home and told my wife I was heading back to San Francisco for Malcolm's event, Jen—perhaps feeling I'd surrender to wild, gay abandon in a room full of chubby brothers—said she was going to come with me. So I bought three tickets to Oakland on Southwest Airlines: one for me, one for Jen, one empty seat so we didn't have to sit with any strangers. Simple.

Simple started shitting itself pretty quickly. That morning, Jen opted to not make the trip to San Francisco, insisting I simply turn around and fly home after the IBR. So I dragged my ass to the Burbank airport and stuck my ID in the machine to retrieve my ticket to Oakland. That's when the machine spit out *two* tickets: one for me, and one for an extra seat—the seat that would've been between me and Jen had she traveled with me as intended, keeping our row somewhat private. Traveling alone, however, I had no need for this extra ticket. But as I was running late for the flight, rather than turn in the second ticket for a refund, I opted to eat the cost and head to the plane.

The flight was pretty empty, so not only did I not need my second seat, many passengers had whole *rows* to themselves. We landed in Oakland without incident and I cabbed it over to the hotel that was ground zero for the International Bear Rendezvous, where Malcolm and I did a gay bear/straight bear podcast for a ballroom full of heavy dudes like us (as well as some of the twinks who eat them).

So it was a fat, fat day. I was among my people: jolly dudes—except these dudes were particularly jolly because they like sucking cock a whole bunch. And while we weren't championing morbid obesity, shouting from stage, "Let's celebrate our unhealth! It's cool to be fat!" we also weren't mourning being out of shape, as if being portly is a debilitating handicap. Some of us would rather concentrate on the engine that drags the rest of that cellulite-packed train. For me, the year leading up to this day was more about taking care of the upstairs than the downstairs, so to speak: recharging the batteries, rebooting the software, chasing whimsies. I wasn't thinking about getting out and exercising every (or any) day; I was figuring out what to do with myself in a world where I knew I didn't want to direct many more films. Trimmer thighs don't seem that important when there are bigger issues and concerns on your mind.

But IBR was refreshing—it was the one place where being fat was celebrated. I live my life fat and I have to navigate through a thin person's world at all times, and if you want to do that without vocal ridicule from the normies, you've always gotta offer them empty reassurance that you're trying to do something about your weight problem. If they feel like you're at least sorry for your grievous offense of not looking like everybody else, they'll leave you alone. At least until they need to make sport of you to raise themselves up a bit at a social gathering, where folks can watch you react to the last acceptable prejudice in this country: fat bias. It's a world full of size queens, and folks who look like me tend to get the hairy eyeball for not being able to maintain a shape or form that's easy on the eyes for the fit 'n' trim to have to look at.

After the gay ol' times of the live *SModcast* at the International Bear Rendezvous were over, I took a cab to the airport. I was booked on a seven-ish o'clock flight. I still had two seats for the flight back. Southwest flights from Oakland to Burbank run hourly, and I was very early for my flight. So I figured I'd try to get on the 5:20 flight back to Los Angeles and my wife. I'd been surrounded by big, hairy dudes who look like me all afternoon, and it was time to get home and fuck the tall, skinny, dickless Schwalbach.

I went up to the counter and asked, "Is it possible to go standby on an earlier flight?" The lady at the ticketing counter was beyond irritated that I'd asked her to perform a tortuous task that's likely explained in detail in her job description: help the customers, especially when they ask for your assistance.

Very disinterested, she handed me a slip of paper. "Here's a pass that'll get you down to the gate. They have to do it there."

Likely because of the weak economy, not every gate has its own dedicated check-in desk anymore. Instead of every gate having a desk and an attendant or two, Southwest in Oakland has a desk that serves three different gates. It makes little sense: two people behind the counter serving three flights full of a hundred and fifty to two hundred people apiece, each with tons of questions, some trying to get on standby.

"I'm trying to get on the five twenty, and they gave me

this card that just says, 'Hand over for boarding pass,' " I said when I finally got up to the counter. "Do I do that now?"

Without even being offered a cursory glance, I was told, "No, you're fine."

"They told me I was on a list up front. I just want to make sure I'm on that list. Because if a standby seat opens up, I really wanna get home."

After I was assured I was on the list, I grabbed a personal pie from a California Pizza Kitchen express. I ate less than half, rolling over in my head, "That person who dealt with me before barely looked at me. Maybe I'll try the other one . . ."

So I approached the counter again, and admittedly, I was acting like I hadn't had the first conversation at the desk when I said, "Hi—am I on a list or something like that?"

The Southwest employee at the check-in desk? Let's call her Ms. Panic. Ms. Panic said, "You are on a list but it's a very, very packed flight. If everyone checks in, there's only gonna be one extra seat left."

"Great, I'll take it!" I said. "I've got tickets for two seats, but I'm happy to do a single seat if I can go home on an earlier flight."

And Ms. Panic looked at me, trying to express something very foreign to a nonterrorist such as myself. "Well, there's the other issue. The safety issue."

We were at an airport and she introduced the term *safety.* So naturally, I asked, "Al-Qaeda?"

"No—your armrests have to be able to . . ." Ms. Panic struggled to find the term.

I was so confused, I asked, "Am I sitting next to a door?

You need me to open the door if the plane goes down? I can do that. I'm ready. If I'm alive after the crash, I'll happily open the door for everybody."

But that's not what it was. As she looked at me, tongue tied by corporate-speak, I recognized the expression on her face as one I'd been at the receiving end of many times over the course of my blubbery existence: She was a thin person dealing with a fat person, marveling over how the chubby had let himself go so badly.

"Oh—you think I bought two tickets 'cause I'm fat," I said. "Ma'am, I am fat. I'll be the first to tell you I'm fat, but I ain't *that* fat yet—where I gotta buy two seats to fly on Southwest. I don't buy two tickets because of my weight; I just don't like people. I don't wanna have to sit next to strangers. So please: If there is one seat, don't worry about my other one. I just wanna get home."

Her mouth said, "Okay," but her face and body language screamed, "Fat's fat, you fat piece of shit." See, to thin people, all of us fat people look alike: We're pigs who pile on more calories than we burn. Within the world of the eternally hungry, we tend to be a bit more understanding of uncontrollable urges and weakness of willpower. We even have acceptable degrees of obesity, so we *know* when we've passed *our* comfort number on the scale—a line that ranges far wider than it does for the normies. Thin folks would see ten pounds in a month as unacceptable weight gain. Fat people go for larger, rounder numbers: Fifty, one hundred, or two hundred pounds of weight gain is where we start to accept we've failed at fitness. Meanwhile, the bony world can't process how lazy and insatiable we chubsters must be, as we don't seem to notice we've let ourselves go. Believe me, Skinny Minnies: We *know.* It's the bane of our existence. But in order to keep our sanity and dignity, we move the line for ourselves much more liberally than the First Lady and Richard Simmons would like us to. It's a matter of survival.

Most Americans are always looking to lose a few pounds, but fat folks spend their *lives* on a never-ending diet. Right about then, I was wishing I could've told these sizes queens and their bullshit, fat-cist airline to kick fucking rocks while I leapt atop Fat-cor, the pudgy dog-dragon, and took off into friendlier skies. Instead, I was forced to deal with Southwest Airlines, hoping there might be less judgment and more customer service somewhere in that plastic heart of a logo they stand behind.

So as the flight was about to close, Ms. Panic practically whispered, "Kevin Smith," over the loudspeaker. Since I'm listening closely, I hear it and race to the desk. I hand over my two tickets and they hand me back two pieces of paper: One is my boarding pass, the other is a drink ticket. Southwest boards in letter groups, so if you pay an additional few bucks, you get to board earlier and they give you a free drink on the plane.

Ms. Panic handed me two documents, but only one of them was a boarding pass. I gave her two boarding passes for my later flight; she gave me one boarding pass and a drink ticket for the standby flight.

"This is only one boarding pass," I said. "I had two tickets."

"There's only one seat left on the plane," she snapped.

"I understand—but what do I do about the other ticket that I had?"

"There's only one seat," she said, waving me toward the Jetway ten or twenty yards from the counter. "Just get on the plane. You're gonna miss the plane. The door's gonna close."

So finally, I put my foot down in the most polite way I could. I am, after all, representing my parents out here in the world, and Mom and Dad always told me, "Everyone deserves to be heard." Years later, I'd add to that sentiment, ". . . no matter how crazy or full of shit they are."

I'm not a confrontational or rude guy: "Death before discourtesy" is on my family's coat of arms. But while I was raised very well, my manners don't come from a completely altruistic place either: I just never want to give anyone cause to mutter, "There's that fuckin' *Clerks*-guy asshole . . ." Folks tend to resent you if you're one of those people who desires more than you're given in life, and they hate it even more when you're willing to work to make it a reality.

So I looked Ms. Panic in her harried, stressed-out eyes and went human being on her: "Ma'am, I understand the plane is leaving. I'm just looking for a little information here: I gave you two tickets, now I have one ticket. Where'd that money go?"

"It'll just be credited to your account! Just go!" she barked at me, not even making eye contact. I hadn't asked her to illustrate the Pythagorean theorem, I merely inquired about my second ticket—and here she is, snapping at me. It was so deflating and irritating.

But rather than snap right back at her, I went all Spock calm, reminding Ms. Panic, "I'm only asking a question, ma'am—about tickets I paid for already."

She offered a halfhearted apology for being so brusque

and sent me to the plane. Once I was in the Jetway, there was a Southwest employee heading toward me with a clipboard. His expression was not warm as he asked me, "Whoa, whoa—who are you?"

"I'm the standby guy. They said I could board."

And he said, "Well, are you memmememue?"

I couldn't understand the last word in his sentence, so I sputtered something about not being clear on what he said. He called out to the guy taking tickets at the top of the Jetway, "Is this guy memmememue?"

"What's that word mean, man?" I asked, befuddled, then tagged it with a joke to keep everyone in this apparently very stressful situation calm. "Am I being reclassified as fuckin' luggage?"

Suddenly, Mr. Jetway turned into Mr. Hyde.

"What'd you say?!" he snapped, reacting as if I'd asked instead, "Can I shit in your mouth and fuck your wife or loved one?"

I repeated the joke, which is never a good sign: "Am I being reclassified as luggage, dude?"

Mr. Jetway stared at me coldly for a beat, then muttered, "I said *revenue*."

"What does *revenue* mean?" I knew the traditional definition of the term, of course—just not the bullshit, corporate double-speak definition as bastardized by Southwest Airlines.

"*Revenue* means it's not an air miles pass," he said, offering the information as if I'd slapped it out of his nuts with a cruise ship mooring rope. "It means you paid for your ticket."

"Then I'm revenue," I proclaimed proudly, trying to lighten the mood. "I paid for my ticket."

"He's revenue," Mr. Jetway told the friendly young flight attendant waiting in the doorway of the plane, who lit up like Christmas upon recognizing me.

"This is so cool!" she said in a respectful whisper as the happy camper headed back up the Jetway (at a suspiciously brisk pace).

I walked onto the plane and it was packed. Everybody else was already aboard, and there was only one open seat remaining: up front in the first row on the right-hand side. There were two very slight women already sitting in the three-seat row, with one empty seat between them, and one was an adorable, squishy old grandma, just a big, smiley prune, happy to still be aboveground. Older than fuck but adorable. The other woman seemed indifferent to my presence and maybe just a little disappointed that her empty seat buffer was disappearing. *"Hello!"* cooed the squishy old lady in such a way that I realized the entire hour-long flight was going to be spent listening to my aged seatmate reminisce about her first flight years prior with her college pals Orville and Wilbur.

I offered her a return greeting as I got ready to buckle my seat belt. It took a degree of sucking in the gut, but nothing troubling or noticeable to anyone but me, and no extender was required. Once the metal fastener caught and closed, I would not only be able to exhale, I could eat the free peanuts they'd be whipping around the cabin later, too.

That was when I saw Ms. Panic heading down the Jetway toward the door of our plane, eyes locked on me. She was so intense and full of purpose, for some strange reason, I assumed she was coming to inform me that my mother had died.

"Mr. Smith. Hi." Ms. Panic smiled as she crouched in front of me in the bulkhead, once she was on the plane. "Um . . . we have kind of a problem . . ."

"My mother died?" I said, finishing her thought. Her eyes flashed momentary confusion at my assumption, until she remembered why she was really there.

"No," Ms. Panic said in a quiet voice. "The captain says that you can't sit here."

"Why?" I asked. And I was *really* asking, because I had no clue. It never occurred to me this was a weight-related issue because I'm not the size normally deemed problematic in matters of public transportation.

And as delicately as she could put it in front of the two women sitting on either side of me who were now under the assumption they were sitting beside a terrorist, Ms. Panic said, "Well, no. It's just, it's a safety issue. It's a security measure."

"Wait—safety? Security?" I asked, suddenly flipping the script and wondering if Ms. Panic was actually some kind of female Jack Bauer, trying to save *me* from the mother/daughter tag-team terrorists sitting on either side of me. And as I mentally prepared to go all Sam Jackson on these would-be, distaff troublemakers in travelers' clothing flanking me and get these motherfuckin' *mothers* off that motherfuckin' plane . . . Ms. Panic lowered the boom. Or the armrests, as it were.

"Mr. Smith, if you can't lower the armrests, then we're not . . . We can't let you . . ."

And after a second, I understood what she was getting at; this was, after all, the woman who had already profiled me earlier. What she *wanted* to say but couldn't was, "We think you're too fat to fly, so you have to buy two seats. But this flight's already oversold and you can't buy an additional seat right now, so you're gonna have to get off the plane. In front of all these people."

That was when the terror crashed over me like a wave: the sinking feeling that everyone was seeing this and everyone was guessing what the flight attendant was talking to me about. And as if I was coping with the death of my dignity at the hands of this uniformed quarter-pounder working for a corporation that can barely mask its utter contempt for the overweight, I went through most of Kübler-Ross's stages of grief—the first being denial.

"This can't be happening," I said to Ms. Panic. "Look— the armrest can go down, ma'am!" And I lowered and lifted the armrests to support my claim.

"I'm sorry," she offered. "Captain's orders."

The next stage for me was bargaining, as I turned to the women on either side of me for support against the mongrel horde.

"Ask these ladies!" I said, turning to the middle-aged woman sitting on my left. "Ma'am, am I squishing you?"

"It's only an hour flight," was her response. Not exactly the ringing endorsement I was looking for, but hey, at this point, I'd have taken any assist I could get.

With that in mind, I turned to the little old lady next to me who couldn't hear shit and asked loudly, "Ma'am, am I squishing you?"

And she asked, "*Whaaaat?*" in such a cartoonishly old-lady fashion, I thought she was gonna reach into her granny bag and pull out one of those ancient hearing aids that looks like those equally ancient phonograph speakers. So I repeated, "*Squiiiishhhh . . . ,*" while making the lemon face and pulling my arms in tightly. Only some half-assed American sign language was gonna get us through this quagmire.

Again, Grandma asked, "*Whaaaat?*"

So at this point, I went for broke: I was making a bigger mime show out of one word than I ever did in six cinematic turns as Silent Bob, almost willing myself into a balled-up sponge, singing, "*Squiiiiiiiiishhhhhhhh . . .*"

Finally, she said, "I'm fine." So I turned back to Ms. Panic and said, "They don't care. They're not complaining."

But Ms. Panic would not be moved on this matter. "Yeah, um, I'm sorry. Please, this is really . . . We'll try to make it up to you at the desk, but the captain needs—"

"The captain can't even see me, ma'am," I protested, indicating the bulkhead wall clearly impeding my view of the cockpit, as well as any pilot's supposed corresponding view of me not fitting into my seat. "I was in my seat for twelve seconds when *you* came all the way down from your station to my seat on the plane. I had literally *just* sat down, and I couldn't see the cockpit. If I can't see the cockpit, then how could the *pilot* see me to make this determination at all?"

I leaned all the way across the woman sitting to my left to illustrate how even then, the pilot and I couldn't see each other, but Ms. Panic's expression never changed to indicate compassion or understanding. "The captain's saying you've got to get up, sir."

And this was the moment I dropped any indignation and give her the next Kübler-Ross stage: depression.

"Please don't do this to me, ma'am . . . ," I said, realizing

I was at the mercy of an institutional mentality. "There were people who recognized me when I got on the plane. Everybody will see."

I might as well have been talking to the toilet in the three-inch airplane bathroom. Ms. Panic simply smiled at me blankly and held the company line. I realized I had two moves: Either I dig in, refuse to get up, and defiantly keep the seat I paid for, or I bail as instructed. All that was running through my head now was, "Everybody's gonna know. Everybody on this plane is gonna see me stand, collect my bag, and get off this plane, and they're either gonna assume I'm too fat or guess I'm a shoe bomber!" I wanted to say, "Go get the captain!" but it's tough to kick up a fuss on *any* post-9/11 flight. You could end up Tased by an undercover air marshal or take a fork in the neck from a vigilant passenger. If I got lippy, they might have used that dog stick on me with the neck loop on the end.

I didn't go all Ben Kingsley in *Sexy Beast*, calling out during my forced exit, "I hope this crashes into the sea!" Instead, I quietly got up and moved to collect my bag from the overhead compartment across the aisle. But as I did this, I made perfect eye contact with a man three rows behind me who was *far* fatter and wider than I am—and he was also squeezed into a middle seat.

I could've pointed out my brother from a fatter mother. "*What about tubby?*" I could've bellowed. "He's twice the man that I am!" But I would never throw a fellow fatty under the bus—or the plane, as it were—so I said nothing. But in the moment our eyes locked, the windows to his soul were filled with fear, and he was desperately, wordlessly begging me, "Please don't tell I'm fat . . . Please don't tell

I'm fat . . ." He saw a chubby taken away in shame, and it filled him with terror. "It's finally happened! They're comin' for the fatties! They're taking us to Candyland to kill us all!"

It was time for the final Kübler-Ross stage: acceptance. I collected my bag and disembarked, waiting just outside the door for Ms. Panic. After five minutes of waiting, I slowly headed up the Jetway, dragging my bag behind me pathetically. I waited by the desk for Ms. Panic to emerge from the plane. And waited. And waited. I looked at my phone: Eight minutes I waited.

That's when I realized I'd forgotten a key Kübler-Ross stage . . .

Anger.

Oooh, I was pissed now, and getting even more so. I honestly feel like the old Kevin Smith died on that plane, prior to disembarking. You don't *ever* treat a paying customer the way they treated me that evening. And I realize that sounds ironic coming from the guy who made *Clerks*, the tagline for which was, "Just because they serve you doesn't mean they like you." Irony aside, I wanted satisfaction fast, or I was gonna unleash the kraken.

Ms. Panic finally got back to the desk, all polite smiles, saying, "I'm sorry about that . . ."

"Ma'am, what's the name of the pilot?" I asked, tapping at the keys of my iPhone's memo pad. "The pilot who said I was too fat to fly."

"Nobody said that . . . ," she countered at the counter.

But I had a pretty good counter of my own ready to go. "Then why am I off the plane?"

"Nobody said you were fat, sir . . ." Ms. Panic rolled her eyes.

"Then why was I pulled off the plane?" I demanded.

"There were safety concerns," Ms. Panic repeated.

"What safety concerns are you talking about?!" I barked in a composed manner.

"There is a space allotment for each seat, and you were taking up more than your space allotment."

And I said, "Just say *fat*."

"I didn't say *fat*," she said. "That's your word, not mine." They're so terrified of lawsuits, they phrase the insult they say to your face very carefully as "taking up more than your allotted space." That's just bullshit, PC double-speak for "Hey, you're fat."

I said, "Lady, I'm not gonna sue you for calling me fat. I'm telling you I'm fat. But don't sit here and dance around with euphemisms for fat. Like, just be honest with me."

Instead, she told me, "I can offer you a one-hundred-dollar travel voucher, sir."

"*That's* your idea of making it better?" I asked. "You give me a one-hundred-dollar voucher for humiliating me?"

"Well, what would make it right?" she asked.

"Get me on a helicopter home!" I spat out, only slightly exaggerating. "Or get me on a private jet home! Your airline pulled me off a flight with no reason and embarrassed me while doing it! So make it better!"

After thirty seconds of a blank stare, I told her, "Never mind. Just gimme the pilot's name, ma'am."

"Why?" she asked again.

"Because of the many things I do, I'm kind of a quasi-journalist. And I'm gonna talk about this in a blog or in a podcast, so I need the pilot's name—because you said he booted me off the plane. Is that true?"

"Why would I say that if it wasn't true, sir?"

"I just don't know how the pilot could've seen me. I'd been in my seat for less than a minute and I couldn't see him around the bulkhead."

"There are mirrors on the plane," she argued.

"Yeah—in the *bathroom*," I scoffed. "Ma'am, you still have to tell me why I was ejected from that flight."

"There are safety issues—"

"Ma'am! What does that mean?!" I demanded. "Does that mean I'm gonna explode all over the plane?!"

Sensing she was hitting a wall with me, Ms. Panic called for a manager. When the manager joined us, his expression screamed, "Why did I have to catch this late-in-the-day bullet..." After Ms. Panic gave him the details, Mr. Manager said, "Southwest policy says you have to be seated comfortably with the armrests down."

"But I *could* put the armrests down!" I shot back.

Neither Mr. Manager nor Ms. Panic ever had a response for that. The Southwest "customers of size" policy makes a big deal about the armrests, but that wasn't getting me anywhere with these two, who didn't seem to understand my frustration at all. But how could they? They were both physically fit, and physically fit people don't have a clue how much planning goes into the average chubby funster's day. I would *never* choose a seat if there was a fraction of a chance that I could not fit into it. That's how I live my life! I'm a fat person! We navigate the world differently than other people. We have to think ten steps in advance for the sake of what little dignity we're afforded in this image-conscious, judgmental society.

All I wanted to do was get out of there now, so while I

was waiting for some Southwest satisfaction, I thought about driving home from the Bay Area. I abandoned the idea when I realized the trip would take three times as long as a normal drive, because I'd be pulling over steamy every three minutes to post tweets. "And another thing! Southworst Err-lines can eat my big fat ass!"

Mr. Manager offered me a brochure, saying, "On the back of this is the address for the corporate office. You can write to them with any complaints."

"I don't have to write to Southwest, buddy," I said. "In an hour, Southwest is gonna come looking for *me.*"

I walked away and sat down at another gate, where I started tweeting about the incident, attacking Southwest for their insensitive behavior. If I had any less self-esteem, I would've been in tears, bawling. But I recalled the lessons of childhood and the simple adage my parents used to say to me when I was a grade-schooler:

"If someone fucks you, and you don't wanna be fucked, then tell people: Start screaming."

So I screamed with tweets . . .

Dear @SouthwestAir—I know I'm fat, but was Captain Leysath really justified in throwing me off a flight for which I was already seated? (5:52 PM 02/13/2010)

Dear @SouthwestAir, I flew out in one seat, but right after issuing me a standby ticket, Oakland Southwest attendant told me Captain Leysath deemed me a "safety risk". Again: I'm way fat . . . But I'm not THERE just yet. But if I am, why wait til my bag is up, and I'm seated WITH ARM RESTS DOWN. In front of a packed plane with a bunch of folks who'd already I.d.ed me as "Silent Bob." (5:54 and 5:56 and 5:58 PM 02/13/2010)

So, @SouthwestAir, go fuck yourself. I broke no regulation, offered no "safety risk" (what, was I gonna roll on a fellow passenger?). I was wrongly ejected from the flight. And fuck your apologetic $100 voucher, @SouthwestAir. Thank God I don't embarrass easily (bless you, JERSEY GIRL training). But I don't sulk off either: so every day, some new fuck-you Tweets for @SouthwestAir. (6:00 and 6:03 and 6:06 PM 02/13/2010)

Wanna tell me I'm too wide for the sky? Totally cool. But fair warning, folks: IF YOU LOOK LIKE ME, YOU MAY BE EJECTED FROM @SOUTHWESTAIR. (6:10 PM 02/13 /2010)

@SouthwestAir? You fucked with the wrong sedentary processed-foods eater! (6:18 PM 02/13/2010)

On and on it went as I hammered Southwest Airlines to 1.6 million on Twitter. They embarrassed me, I embarrassed them right back. And while I know that the president of Southwest Airlines didn't boot me off the plane, and while I also know the unlucky soul who runs that Southwest Twitter account didn't red-flag me, if you sling hash for an organization that fucks with me and mine, then you're getting dragged into it, too. Welcome to the party, pal!

And after almost an hour of tweeting, somebody got fuckin' scared shitless—because Mr. Manager came to find me. I saw him race by me at first, clearly on a desperate hunt. Then, when he doubled back, he saw me leaning against a wall across from my new gate. He sprinted over and breathlessly coughed, "Mr. Smith—please stop tweeting!"

He told me I was handled poorly and he wanted to make it up to me by ensuring I got out of Oakland (and tweeting distance) as soon as possible on the next Southwest flight to Burbank. I told him I was already holding section A seats, which would allow me to board first. He offered me the $100 travel voucher again, which I declined, but the dude had his marching orders, and they were to get me on another Southwest flight home, ASAP. So even though I insisted on boarding when my section was called, Mr. Manager escorted me onto the next flight when the doors opened— which was embarrassing because everyone else in line stared. And even though I had the whole plane to choose from, I immediately hurled my fat ass into the first available seat: a window seat in the bulkhead, this time on the other side of the plane. When I got onto that flight, the most important thing in the world to me was buckling my seat belt without incident.

As the rest of the passengers boarded, I read all the response tweets and Twitter reactions to my earth-scorching Southwest diatribe. While I was being force-boarded onto my flight home, Southwest Airlines reached out via Twitter, asking me to get in touch with them. So I tweeted some more . . .

Dear @SouthwestAir, I'm on another one of your planes, safely seated & buckled-in again, waiting to be dragged off in front of the normies. (6:41 PM 02/13/2010)

And, hey? @SouthwestAir? I didn't even need a seat belt
extender to buckle up. Somehow, that shit fit over my "safety
concern"-creating gut. (6:41 PM 02/13/2010)

Via @bogo_lode "Maybe you should organize a boycott." A
boycott of one. This is my last Southwest flight. Hopefully by
choice. (6:46 PM 02/13/2010)

I snapped a picture of myself with my camera phone and
tweeted what became a very popular image accompanying
every rendition of this story: me in one seat, puffing out my
cheeks to look fatter. I included the message . . .

Hey @SouthwestAir! Look how fat I am on your plane!
Quick! Throw me off! http://twitpic.com/1340gw (6:52 PM
02/13/2010)

I continued tweeting until takeoff . . .

Hey @SouthwestAir! Sometimes, the arm rests are up because THE PEOPLE SITTING THERE ALREADY PUT THEM
UP; NOT BECAUSE THEY "CAN'T GO DOWN." (6:56 PM
02/13/2010)

The @SouthwestAir Diet. How it works: you're publicly
shamed into a slimmer figure. Crying the weight right off has
never been easier! (6:59 PM 02/13/2010)

While I was tweeting pre-takeoff, a large girl—big like
me—sat near me at the other end of the aisle, with an empty

seat between us. I was thinking, "Did they just create a fat section and put me and this poor girl in it? Have we been profiled?" And I'm tweeting up a storm when I see a flight attendant come over and ask this girl to follow her. They were gone for three minutes, and when the girl returned, she ordered a very stiff drink.

Fifteen minutes before the flight landed, I was buckling up in preparation for landing and the girl and I made casual eye contact. I smiled, she smiled, and then she asked, "Where you going?"

"Home," I yawned. "I've had a horrible experience with this airline today. They just booted me off my last flight because they said I was too fat."

That's when she revealed the heartbreaker. "They just did something like that to me, too—before we took off."

She explained that every time she flew, she chose to sit in the back row so as to be out of plain sight. But as she boarded this flight, she was instructed by the flight attendant to sit in the front row instead—the same row I was in. Then, ten minutes later, she was instructed to follow the flight attendant back out into the Jetway, where she was told, "You should be purchasing an extra seat for travel, ma'am. It's not fair to other passengers."

"You're sitting in a row where there's an empty seat," I pointed out. "I bought two seats."

"The flight attendant said that I would have to ask you if it was okay if I shared your row without buying an extra ticket."

That performance piece, courtesy of the Southwest Players, was intended to show me that *all* fat people get "the talk" at Southwest. How sick is that? They used that poor girl—literally forced her to sit in my row—just so they could pull her off the plane, shame her, and send her back to her seat, crying. They'd hoped I'd hear what happened to her and figure I wasn't being singled out. They tried to make it about fat again, ever covering for the jackasses who colluded to get me off the plane. There was no reason for that flight attendant to have that conversation with that girl except to be a cunt. And the girl was telling me through tears, "I could still put the armrest down." We must've been quite a sight: a couple of chubsy-ubsies talkin' about how proud we were that we could still buckle the seat belt without an extender, and you could tell it was the only shred of dignity we had left.

We landed in Burbank and I remember thinking, "Boy, there better be nineteen fuckin' Southwest Airlines people . . ."

Nothing. Not a goddamn thing. So I tweeted . . .

Hey @SouthwestAir! I've landed in Burbank. Don't worry: wall of the plane was opened & I was airlifted out while Richard Simmons supervised. (8:18 PM 02/13/2010)

It was tough shit making all those fat jokes at my own expense, but I figured it'd be worth it to see this dopey company called on the carpet for fucking over customers, caught by a guy who boasts more Twitter followers than their airline. See, *I* thought the story was about how a corporation got caught fucking over the little guy again, except this time, the little guy had a lot of mouth and even more Twitter followers. But look how long that sentence is. Why the fuck did I expect the media to understand all that when there was an easier, funnier story staring right at them? And that story was *Fat Guy in a Little Chair*!

Almost every news outlet spent three days stripping away my humanity, as people discussed me more like a concept than an individual. My picture graced the *Philadelphia Daily News* with the slug, "Blimp landed." I learned firsthand that fat people are the recipients of the last remaining socially acceptable prejudice. Racism and sexism will get you ostracized in more enlightened communities, but you can mock fat people all you want. I saw some intense hate rhetoric online, all stemming from some subtly antifat propaganda that made me wonder if Goebbels had really died in the bunker, or if he'd ducked out, come to the States, and gotten a job in Dallas, working for an airline.

For three days, I'd wake up and find Jen sifting through Google News, reading all the Too Fat to Fly stories as they accumulated, updating me on the count.

"Four hundred articles now," she'd announce, much to my chagrin. Even worse: "You're also at the top of the news page." Then, two days later: "It's up to five thousand articles and you're *still* at the top of the Google News page."

By the morning after I got back to L.A., there was national TV coverage of the incident, and by midday, the coverage was *international.* Larry King reached out to me via Twitter. Larry King—in his final year in the big broadcast suspenders—invited me to guest on his show and tell the story. For as many times as I'd wished Larry King would've had me on his program to talk about my *art*, here he was reaching out to *me*—via *my* medium of Twitter—to talk about *this* shit. I flashed on a future in which I was the current incarnation of the Octomom, making the media rounds barking about the rights of the morbidly obese while scarfing donuts and plugging my new movie. Or DVD. Or action figure.

So as tempting as it was to be on one of Larry King's last few broadcasts, I opted out of appearing on *Larry King Live* to discuss the Too Fat to Fly incident. I opted out of doing *Good Morning America* as well, but they're the date rapist of morning shows, as far as I'm concerned—because even though I turned down their interview request out of the New York office, they came to my *house* with a camera and knocked on the front door. Hey, *Good Morning America*: Next time I'm not giving you what *you* want, just force my head down there and *make* me do it. How about, in the future, you respect the simple notion of no means no, you fucking pigs?

To be fair, they weren't the *only* media jackasses to "weigh" in on the matter. Dr. Endorsement TV Whore Quack said something. I got no justice from Emaciated Old Woman Fake Judge, who sided with the corporation that advertises on her TV program. *Forbes*, too, circled the wagons around their corporate fuck-buddies at Southwest and wrote that I'd done *myself* more harm than Southwest with this fiasco, hurting my "brand" in the process. I stopped being a person to all of these people. None of them listened to my account of the incident; they all profiled me as fat, hence guilty of this obvious fat crime. Lots of folks online were telling me to stop crying and lose weight. I kept telling them, "I know I'm fat. But I'm not too fat to fly on Southwest Air."

Southwest eventually reached out to me. But they refused to ever admit that I wasn't too fat for the seat. They kept insisting that it was the pilot's decision, and in a post-9/11 world, who the fuck is going to question a pilot when it comes to safety? Eventually they backed off even that claim, saying simply that an employee made the determination I was too fat.

So Big Business won again, spreading the gospel of "Look, I'm Sorry: He's Just Too Fat. And Seriously—Don't We All Hate Fat People Anyway?" I'll carry this shit with me like herpes for the rest of my life, regardless of my waistline size—all because a shitty organization didn't have the simple Southern decency to admit they were wrong.

Hurled from the skies like the son of Odin himself, after the Too Fat to Fly incident, I was understandably hesitant to go near an airport ever again, unless it was to get a Cinnabon. And considering *why* I didn't want to go near an airport, Cinnabons weren't going to play a big role in my life for a while. This was compounded by a posting I read on a paparazzi Web site, offering a bounty for new pictures of Fatty McNoFly in the wild. The price of my further humiliation? Five grand for a picture of me sitting in a little chair, and ten grand if I was also eating a sandwich. And when I go to the airport, all I *do* is sit in little chairs and eat shit.

Being cast out of the heavens is fine if you don't have a shit-ton of Q & A shows scheduled all across the country. Less than three weeks after the Southwest fiasco, I had a pair of gigs in Austin and Houston. The week after that, a show in Milwaukee. The following week was Devils Classic Sweater day back at the Prudential Center in Jersey, and the next week was a George Carlin celebration at the New York Public Library, followed by shows in Detroit and Kansas

City two days later. Tough to get thousands of miles without an airplane. Tough, but not impossible.

So I called around looking for a tour bus I could rent that'd get me to Austin and Houston. The folks at Coast to Coast Coach were helpful at first, then really confused.

"How many people in your band?" I was asked on the phone by the booking agent.

"Just me," I said. "One guy."

"One guy needs a whole tour bus?" the agent asked.

"It's for a spoken-word tour," I said. "I like my space."

There was a pause, and then the voice on the other end of the phone said, "Wait a minute . . . are you that Too Fat to Fly guy?"

In the two years since the fake-heart fascists added Chubby-Hater to their list of sky offenses, Southwest Airlines has ejected *more* people from their planes: A member of the band Green Day was kicked off one of their flights for wearing baggy pants, and months later, Southwest booted a star of Showtime's *The L Word* because she was kissing her girlfriend. I used to think Southwest just had an issue with fat people, but it became clear that they don't like anyone *different.* If you're fat, slack, or gay as the day is long, it would seem you're not always welcome on their planes. That's okay: Last year, while in midflight, a hole ripped open in the ceiling of a Southwest jet. Call me Too Fat to Fly all you want, but I call *that* Too *Fucked* to Fly. When an airplane's roof opens in midair, not even the forced purchase of *two* seats will save your life.

But, as with all of life's big, bad boo-boos, I'd have to say it was Mom who ultimately made it all better. A day after I was deemed Too Fat to Fly, my mother sent me an e-mail, reminding me why I was in this mess in the first place: Not because I'm *fat*, but because the big guy (ironically *not* me in this case) fucked the little guy (somehow me)—plain and simple.

"LOVE YOU VERY MUCH," Mom wrote. "MAKE POP HAPPY. A POOR POSTAL WORKER'S SON GOES POSTAL ON SOUTHWEST AIRLINES. HAHA."

Not a bad bit of biting social satire from a woman who yelled at my dad once for letting twelve-year-old me watch *Carlin at Carnegie.*

CHAPTER THIRTEEN

Funny as Shit

They say you should never meet your heroes. For an all-too-brief moment in time, they could've amended that sentiment to include the caveat ". . . unless your hero is George Carlin."

My first exposure to the Smartest Man I Ever Met was through his albums. My father worked the night shift at the post office, and on his dinner breaks, he'd buy used records from a coworker's car trunk: country albums for him, comedy records for his kid. Bill Cosby was a staple and easy to get by my mother, as Cosby never worked blue. But one morning when he came home from work, my father gave me an album while I was still in bed.

"Don't show your mother," he cautioned me. "She's not ready for this."

But *I* was. I'd become a huge fan of language and writing

by age twelve, and Dad recognized the intelligence of Carlin's—so much so that he wanted to impart it to his preteen boy, much in the same way sports-fan fathers like to share a beer with their boys while watching the big game, even if they're not of drinking age. Dad felt Carlin was onto something new, real, and relevant with his comedy, and he thought it was necessary to share it with his comedy-cravin' kid, blue language be damned. So even though we were a church-every-Sunday Catholic family of five, here was my father suborning subversion.

And with good reason: As I spun *Class Clown* for the first time, I was *transfixed*. This man Carlin spoke the truth, but more important, he was hysterical while doing so—a funny prophet. *FM & AM* and *Class Clown* became as memorized and shared in my world as any *Monty Python* routine or *Saturday Night Live* sketch. And in the Catholic school world of Our Lady of Perpetual Help, being able to quote a Carlin bit was pure pop-culture currency.

In 1982, HBO aired the *Carlin at Carnegie* stand-up special. A commercial for the premiere featured a clip of Carlin talking about the clichéd warning to criminals, "Don't try anything funny . . ."

"When they're not looking," he added mischievously, "I like to go . . ."

BOOM! George disappeared into an explosion of goofy expressions and pantomime so wild and woolly, you half expected the Tasmanian Devil to be standing there when he finally stopped. It was the missing piece in all those comedy albums I'd been listening to: I could *see* the brilliance now as well. Carlin used his body like an instrument onstage, creating noises, striking poses, and treading the boards with all the passion of a preacher, but none of the irritating piety.

I was about to ask my parents if I could tape the comedy special on our brand-new Betamax video recorder when my old man pulled me aside and said, "George Carlin's gonna be on the HBO this weekend."

So we sat down to watch it that weekend evening: my dad, my mom, and me. During the cold opening where George talks about the old joke "How do you get to Carnegie Hall?" ("Practice, man. Practice"), my mother checked one last time with my dad.

"You sure this is okay for him to watch?" she asked, handing her third child—the *plump* one—a Swanson's dinner in front of the TV.

"Sure," Dad replied, forking through an Apple Brown Betty. "Carlin's a Catholic."

George Carlin, we'd soon learn together as a family, was a *recovering* Catholic. *Big* difference . . .

So there I was, lying on my stomach on the floor, eyes on HBO, waiting for my TV dinner to cool down. There was my father, sitting on the couch to my right. My mother was sitting to my left, in an aged recliner we called the Big Chair. And on TV was some magical place in New York City I'd heard Bugs Bunny mention in a cartoon once, making it as unreal as Pismo Beach or Albuquerque. But while he was crafty and cool as Bugs, George Carlin was real—which meant Carnegie Hall had to be as well.

And George Carlin stepped out onto the Carnegie Hall stage and made it all *way* more real with his opening line.

"Have you ever noticed that people who are against abortion are people you wouldn't wanna fuck in the first place?"

As you might imagine, there were two different parental reactions to that joke: hysterics from Dad, horror from Mom.

"Turn it off!" Mom said in that Mom-Don't-Like voice.

"Oh, why?" my dad countered. "He's totally fine." And then turning to me, he asked, "You think this is too grown-up for you?"

"Mom"—I turned to her over my left shoulder, mustering as much earnestness as I could—"what's abortion?"

"You're on your own, Don . . . ," she barked, heading to the kitchen. "Have fun explaining all the curses to your youngest son!"

He would've, I'm sure, but he knew he wouldn't have to. Of course I knew all the curse words; I was a Catholic school student.

George Carlin was the first person who ever said *fuck* in my house. Back in the day, the movies didn't feature that word so prominently; and *nobody* in my house was allowed to use vulgarity. But here was this intelligent, articulate, thinking man who wielded the word like a rapier—and *that* was suddenly permitted. The lesson: You can curse if you've also got an impressive vocabulary to choose from. The conventional wisdom had always been, "People who swear are uneducated and lazy." This guy Carlin proved you can know a shit-ton of words—you could even command the English language like you'd found its magic lamp—and *still* opt to employ the occasional (or frequent) F-bomb. Someone cursing didn't make my father laugh; someone cursing while being humorously truthful could make my father cry laughing. Duly noted.

I was twelve years old watching a man many years my senior curse a blue streak while exposing the hypocrisy of a medium (and a society) that couldn't deal with the public usage of terms they probably employed regularly in their private lives. And while he seemed to revel in being a rebel, here was a man who also clearly loved the English language, warts and all—even the so-called bad words (although, as George would say, there are no such things as "bad words"—only bad intentions). I wouldn't say George Carlin taught me obscenities, but I would definitely say he taught me that the casual use of obscenities wasn't reserved for just drunken sailors.

And that was *before* he got to the seven words you can't say on television . . .

But more than the naughty words, I loved Carlin's freedom: Whether he was spinning a yarn about Tippy, his farting dog, or analyzing the contents of his fridge, Carlin expressed himself not only humorously but amazingly eloquently as well. He was a nimble public speaker who never excluded you, even if he was making fun of a common human foible you share with many others. But whatever he spoke about, you got the impression he was getting away with something—saying things others may have wanted to but couldn't, or weren't allowed to, or were simply too nervous about expressing themselves to say. He was having a good time being himself *for* the audience, and the audience loved him for being *exactly* who he was: the guy not afraid to mix fart jokes with biting social commentary or simple observations.

And he went high and low: jokes about hypocrisy and jokes about Rice Krispies. While he mimed floating proudly in milk, Mom rejoined us, giggling. This man Carlin was a *magician*: He could relate to smart cats like my dad, Catholic cats like my mom, and everybody in between—including (and maybe in this instance, *especially*) twelve-year-old comedy nerds.

After *Carlin at Carnegie*, I became a disciple (believe me, if I could've followed him around like he was Phish or the Grateful Dead, I'd have gone for apostle). I bought every album, watched every HBO special, and even sat through *The Prince of Tides* just because he played a small role in the film. I spent years recruiting friends into the cult of Carlin and even made pilgrimages to see him perform live (the first live gig I attended being a college show he did at Fairleigh Dickinson University in 1988). Carlin influenced my speech and my writing. Carlin replaced Catholicism as my religion. Carlin was the person I most wanted to be when I grew up.

Sixteen years later, I sat across from the star of *Carlin at Carnegie* in the dining room of the Four Seasons Hotel in Los Angeles. It was a meeting I'd dreamed of and dreaded simultaneously. George Carlin was the type of social observer/critic I most wanted to emulate . . . but he was a celebrity, too. What if he turned out to be a true prick?

What I quickly discovered was that in real life George was . . . well, George. Far from self-obsessed, he was mild-mannered enough to be my dad. He was as interested as he was interesting, well-read, and polite to a fault—all while casually dropping F-bombs. But most impressive, he didn't treat me like an audience member, eschewing actual conversation and electing, instead, to simply *perform* the whole meeting. He talked to me like one of my friends would talk to me: familiar, unguarded, authentic.

He liked the script for *Dogma*, a flick in which I was asking him to play Cardinal Glick—the pontiff-publicist responsible for the Catholic Church's recall of the standard crucifix in favor of the more congenial, bubbly Buddy Christ. He told me he was flattered, as the content made him feel like a spiritual godfather to the script. I confirmed that he was.

"Well, I'll tell ya," he said. "I'd really like to do this. But there's something I'm gonna need."

Money. Here it comes: George Carlin is a capitalist pig. I readied myself for a letdown.

Instead, he stole my heart.

"My wife just died," he said, twisting his wedding band. "And I'm not ready to take my ring off yet. But you want me to play a cardinal. So I was hoping you'll let me wear a Band-Aid over my wedding ring."

At that moment, I'd have let him be my dad, if he'd asked. I loved George Carlin even more for loving his late wife.

I made three films with Carlin over the course of the next six years, starting with *Dogma*. A few years later, I wrote him a lead role in *Jersey Girl* as Pop—the father of Ben Affleck's character. It called for a more dramatic performance than George was used to giving, but the man pulled it off happily and beautifully (something most folks probably don't know about George: He took acting very seriously). Sadly, I consider that *Jersey Girl* part my one failing on George's behalf—not for the reasons most would assume (the movie was not reviewed kindly, to say the least). No, I failed because George had asked me to write a *different* role for him.

In 2001, George did me a solid when he accepted the part of the orally fixated hitchhiker who knew exactly how to get a ride in *Jay and Silent Bob Strike Back*. When he wrapped his scene in that flick, I thanked him for making the time. He said, "Just do me a favor: Write me my dream role one day." When I asked what that'd be, he smiled and said, "I wanna play a priest who strangles six children."

It was a classic Carlin thing to say: a little naughty and a lot honest. And I always figured there'd be time to give George what he asked for, but unfortunately, he left too soon.

On June 17, 2009, it was *my* turn to play Carnegie Hall. It was a very cool accomplishment to even get *booked* into the grand old barn, but I *know* me: If I walked out and saw empty seats, I wouldn't feel as accomplished. I'd just sold out some dates up in Toronto, and if I didn't sell out Carnegie Hall, I might be forced to expatriate, as clearly the True North really liked whatever bullshit I was slinging.

So I started publishing a daily update of ticket sales— something a bunch of folks warned me against. For fringe /cult acts like me, ticket sales info is *closely* guarded data, because perception is power. If you know a band has only sold a quarter of the seats available at their forthcoming concert you're thinking of attending, you may be swayed out of your potential purchase by hearing the show's selling poorly—or at least feel no pressure to purchase tickets in advance. When you don't buy tix in advance, your chances of actually mustering up the interest to leave the house come show day will almost certainly wane.

But here was the tough shit: I knew the only way I was gonna sell out Carnegie Hall was with *help*. So every day, I updated the ticket tally, showing what a game of inches it was to get to twenty-eight hundred seats sold. It didn't help that the economy was in the toilet as we were asking sixty dollars per ticket for what sounded pretty bland. I could see some troll online: "Paying to see a Q & A? Yawn, as well as an in-advance meh . . ."

It took many weeks and a shit-ton of tweets, but on the day of the show, producer Jared Geller told me that walk-up purchases pushed the gig to a sellout at the venerable old theater. As I stepped onstage that night, I did a completely uncharacteristic leap-and-land thing that was born of relief and joy: The selling was behind me—it was time to have some *fun*. It was time to talk about breaking a toilet on the world's most famous stage.

As cliché as it sounds, the whole show's a blur. I recall tidbits: being nervous at first; the aforementioned celebratory leap nearly costing me a knee; talking about people I dearly love and knowing they heard their names bandied about in a cornerstone of high society, which we redefined that night; wrapping up by pointing out my mother and my wife sitting near each other in the audience, observing, "There's the pussy I came from, and there's the pussy I go to." But the rest of the show? A blank.

After the show, my mom came up to me and I thought I was about to get smacked for the crack I'd made during the show. Instead, she rubbed my head as if I wasn't thirty-eight at the time, gazing at me with glassy eyes. She didn't have to say anything; I knew what she was thinking.

"Dad would've liked?" I asked.

"Dad would've loved." She smiled. Then, she added for good measure, "And George would've been proud of you, too."

That night, as I left the stage, I took a picture. Whenever something got me down, or whenever someone tried to make me feel I was less than someone else (or in the case of one classless piece-of-shit airline, *more* than someone else), I'd look at it as a reminder that nobody is allowed to tell me who I am and what I'm worth. I'm including it here for everyone to see . . . and use. Are you trying to get somewhere? *Do* something? *Be* somebody? It can get frustrating waiting for *your* time—particularly because there'll be no end of panty-puddles telling you, "It can't be done!" Or "If it is to be done, you're not the person to do it!" Or the ever-popular "Who the fuck do you think you are? I mean, you're fat." All variations of the will-killing "*Why?*"

If you get frustrated, simply glance at this image of the crowd at Carnegie Hall. Sure, it's something *I* did; but it could easily represent what you're *going* to do. And when you look at this image in a time of need, remind yourself that all of those people packed into that frame, hootin' and hollerin'? They're doing so for a very average, overweight white boy from a Nowheresville, New Jersey, town who got on that stage and induced that reaction simply by being himself. A fat, lazy slob who done good.

So be yourselves, kids.

CHAPTER FOURTEEN

My Wife Is the Shit

In order for you to ascend, someone somewhere has to descend. In order for you to have so much, someone somewhere has to have far less. Someone has to sacrifice in order for you to succeed—even the audience, which gives up its money for your art.

The anonymity of the people making those sacrifices protects you from knowing where the money you make actually comes from, as well as keeps secret all the stories of what folks had to give up just so you can express yourself through art for a living. If I knew how much each dollar spent on crap I produced was actually worth—the effort that went into earning enough money to buy a ticket to a movie I made or purchase a book I wrote—the crushing guilt would likely send me off a cliff. Mercifully, I don't have to see the sacrifices others make so that I can be me for a living.

But here's the tough shit: Sometimes, you come to know the people who've lost something so that you could gain. Sometimes, you know them *intimately.* Sometimes, they tell you to put the toilet seat down when you're finished taking a whiz, or maybe they give birth to your only child.

When I met Jen Schwalbach, I was in awe of her career. She was a twenty-six-year-old writing for *USA Today,* the most widely read newspaper in the known universe. You'd think it was her centerfold looks that captured my fancy, but fat dudes see *lots* of pretty women every day and we don't go to pieces. This is because we're trained by society and the media to believe thin, pretty women are meant for our physical betters: dudes with abs. Skinny, good-looking chicks rarely choose the corpulent fella unless you're watching a sitcom. Jen was (and remains) beautiful and alluring, but that's not what made her interesting to me; it was the fact that, at such a young age, she had what I considered a kick-ass job, where she was influencing millions of people a day.

The universe threw us together for the purposes of spin control: The legend of Ben Affleck and Matt Damon was in danger, and I was charged with setting the record straight. In the run-up to the announcement of the 1998 Academy Award nominations, *Good Will Hunting* was looking like a strong contender for a slew of nods. But the other studios running flicks that year didn't like dem apples at all, so folks took a page out of the Miramax playbook and began pissing in the well, floating a rumor that the boys did *not*, in fact, write *Good Will Hunting* themselves. This was a ludicrous notion if you knew Ben and Matt—which nobody really did at that point. And while human beings can be petty and jealous, human beings who work in the movie biz can be downright Tolkienesque in their quest to see others fail as they reach for *their* ring. The buzz around town was starting to turn from "Have you seen *Good Will Hunting*?!" to "I heard those boys had help with the script."

Two names of secret *Good Will* collaborators were being floated to the press, and while one made sense, the second was ludicrous. William Goldman, the screenwriter of *Butch Cassidy and the Sundance Kid* and *The Princess Bride*, was the first and most believable Cyrano suggested by the competition. Oddly, I was the second name being whispered as a *Good Will* ghostwriter. In any other year, this would have been akin to suggesting I had something to do with *Star Wars* as well. But in April 1997, eight months prior to the *Good Will* opening, Miramax released my third flick: *Chasing Amy*. The more mature style of storytelling in *Amy* coupled with my name on *Good Will Hunting* as a co-executive producer and topped with the fact that both films shared a lead in Affleck spelled collusion to some. As God is my witness, the only hand I had in the script for *Good Will Hunting* was getting the script to Harvey Weinstein. Harvey, in turn, loved *Good Will* and bought the expensive turnaround script from Castle Rock. Ben, Matt, and Harvey asked me to direct it, which seemed equally ridiculous. I said I was flattered but understood they were all largely excited that the flick was finally happening at all, with nobody thinking clearly that a steady, experienced hand should be at the wheel of this potentially mighty ship. I was a dinghy skipper at best.

Goldman, conversely, was a legendary script doctor, and Castle Rock *had* asked the boys to take a meeting with the grand pooh-bah of three-act structure. Castle Rock had bought the spec script for $800,000 and felt the quiet picture about a boy genius whose friends are his safe haven needed some intrigue. There was an NSA subplot the studio was hoping to shoehorn into *Good Will*, spun off the main character's monologue about what might happen should he take the government job he was being offered. The studio was looking for *Hunting Will Hunting*—in which the insidious USA will stop at nothing to get its hands on the Southie savant. During their sit-down, according to Ben and Matt, Goldman told them their script was solid and needed no added bells and whistles. But the fact that the meeting occurred at all was enough to get tongues wagging.

So Gina Gardini, a bionic ninja of a Miramax publicist, tasked me with a mission: give an interview to *USA Today* that would, among other things, allow me a big ol' public forum to deny having anything to do with the writing of *Good Will Hunting*, as well as inform the world that the same script I read on the toilet over two hours, tears streaming down my face, was the same movie Gus Van Sant had made of the boys' script. The ship was listing slightly; I was sent out to right it. Credibility clown pulled on his Miramaxkateer ears and went west.

I was heading to Los Angeles to rehearse *Dogma* with Chris Rock, who was trapped on the set of *Lethal Weapon 4*. Indie producer Scott Mosier had put in a friendly call to Hollywood producer Joel Silver to ask when *Lethal* was dropping Rock, since he was now a week beyond his contractual stop date. Silver screamed at Mos for thirty seconds about how Rock wasn't going anywhere, then—presumably working from a dusty old set of movie-bully sides found in the central casting office of *Lethal* studio Warner Bros.—demanded to know what Mos was gonna *do* about it.

What we did about it was send me to Los Angeles to rehearse *there* with Chris Rock. If Muhammad couldn't get to the mountain, the mountain was gonna come to Muhammad. The timing was perfect because I was going to L.A., anyway, for my first comic book signing. Golden Apple on Melrose was hosting me and artist Jim Mahfood for a *Clerks: The Comic Book* signing, Saturday, January 24, 1998. So Gina Gardini asked if I'd sit down with a journalist from *USA Today* on Friday, January 23. Amid chatter of the upcoming comic book and taking a victory lap for the well-received *Chasing Amy*, I was to remind folks that Ben and Matt had no help in writing *Good Will Hunting*—certainly not from Bill Goldman, and least of all from the likes of me.

"Who am I talking to?" I remember asking Gina.

"Jennifer Schwalbach," Gina said, sounding out the last name that would define the rest of my life.

I'd been in the movie business for four years at that point, so I'd met my share of *USA Today* writers. At that point, they all looked like my mom: older, matronly—even the dudes. So when I married that empirical knowledge to an old-lady-sounding name like Schwalbach, all I was seeing was this midlife giggling Gretel type, whom I'd likely be wrestling with over the last few Pringles in the can.

I was staying at the Bel Age Hotel off Sunset. My Friday was devoted to rehearsing with Rock, interviewing with *USA Today*, and maybe seeing my ex-girlfriend for dinner. Rock came over around noon, and we ran through the entire script together for two hours, stopping only to have getting-to-know-you chitchat about pussy and *Saturday*

Night Live. I said I was hoping to have dinner with my ex-girlfriend, which Rock insisted was a bad idea. She'd moved on, he guessed; better to instead just get laid in L.A. by anybody *but* my ex—that way, I'd get on with my life. We all know Chris Rock's hysterical, but few realize he's also pretty insightful when it comes to relationships.

After our rehearsal, Rock had to go back to the *Lethal Weapon* set for a night shoot. The interview with the reporter who I was sure was going to be older than I was, scheduled for two, so shortly after Rock left, there was a knock at the door. I don't remember much about the walk from the couch to the door, and I wish I'd written it all down, because from the moment I opened that door, everything I thought I knew about life would be challenged and evolved, and everything I was sure I knew about love would suddenly seem childish.

The chick on the other side of the knock at the door didn't look matronly in the least: She was gorgeous, tall, skinny, young—maybe even *my* age. I had spoken with cub reporters before; the Internet was *just* starting to move from the college campuses to homes all across America, and a new kind of journalism allowing for a younger generation of writers and reporters was forming. But print journalism was an old-timers' club back then, so you'd rarely if ever be interviewed by kids your own age.

It is perhaps for this reason, then, that for the first six seconds of the rest of our lives together, I assumed Jennifer Schwalbach was a hooker Chris Rock had sent to my room.

This would explain the pure carnality of our relationship, actually: Since my first impression of my wife-to-be was "sex worker," it would stand to reason that I'm so very physically obsessed with her. Even if we're not in the same room or state, I'm *thinking* about having sex with Jennifer Schwalbach. Put one mile between me and Jen Schwalbach, and there will be phone or iChat sex. This is because the only sexually level playing field for a fat man is in print and on the phone. That's the only way I *ever* got laid in this life: selling my shit with words. In the realm of thoughts and letters, I can be as sexy and seductive as Eric, the vampire Viking in *True Blood.* It's only when I've gotta compete in the visible spectrum that I'm revealed as Jabba the Hutt or Quasimodo.

But there are two ways into any person, body or soul: through the heart and through the head. The eye is less reliable, because it only *sees* — and what we see changes every day. But shit that's lodged in your head or heart? That never goes *anywhere.* It's not visible, so it's an image that's only corrupted by our own folly. The flesh decays, but memories of a feeling, an insight, an intellectual or spiritual impact? They only burn *brighter* with time. We race toward the future while we lionize the past. We look ahead for half our lives, then spend the other half looking back. Written or spoken, words are the foundation of reality, so thankfully, within six seconds of that hotel door swinging wide, the heartbreaker announced her true intentions. "Hi, I'm Jennifer Schwalbach with *USA Today.*"

Those were the first words my wife would ever say to me, thus giving the hook to my Chris Rock hooker theory. I invited her in, repeating over and over how I'd never met anybody from *USA Today* who was younger than Methuselah. She sat on the couch; I sat on the floor opposite her, separated by a coffee table. We covered the *Clerks* comic book, the difference *Amy* made to my career, the burgeoning all-star cast of *Dogma*, and, finally, whether I had anything to do with *Good Will Hunting*. While her mini tape recorder captured my words, it never picked up my *inner* monologue— the bulk of which concerned having such a beautiful, smart, accomplished, interesting, and frighteningly sexy girl in my hotel room, knowing it was going no further than career chitchat. She seemed comfortable in my hotel room, but then chicks usually were around me: Unlike the thin boys who assume every girl wants to fuck them, I'm the nonthreatening chubsy-ubsy—the guy every girl is friends with yet few ever really wanna see naked.

We talked on the record for an hour, and after the interview ended, we talked for two more hours *off* the record. The opening conversation was about the relationships we'd both had a hard time ending, which revealed far more about who we were to each other than a peek inside a diary might've provided. After that, we talked about Los Angeles and how much she loved it, and I talked about Jersey and how I'd never leave it. But mostly, we talked about *her* job. I was blown away that someone so young was writing for the galaxy's most available newspaper. And while we were both in high-profile communications media, the reach she had with her work, I argued, went far further than the reach of my dopey flicks. Her job was ultimately more impressive than mine, so I figured I'd interview *her* for a while. As it turned out, 'til I drop dead.

As she was packing up to head out, Jennifer expressed serious doubt that I spent as much time online answering questions at the Viewaskew.com message board as I said I did. I told her to post a question herself one day and watch

how quickly I responded. We shook hands good-bye—
technically, our first physical intimacy since I can still remember how soft and slender her fingers felt—but I released
quicker than I normally would, so as not to creep her out.
Then, three hours and change after her arrival at my hotel
room door, cub reporter Jen Schwalbach was gone . . .
leaving me six shades of smitten.

All of a sudden, I had this dream of having a girlfriend
as cool and accomplished as Jennifer Schwalbach. The last
time I had a big dream, it was about becoming a filmmaker.
This time, it was about becoming *hers*. And boy, did I *really*
wanna cum with her.

I know I seem fixated on the fluids of it all, but don't let
society fool you: Spermy talk *isn't* immature. Cum's not
only the foundation of life, it's the foundation of any ro-
mantic relationship. People will tell you mutual respect is
what builds bonds, but here's the tough shit: It's really *sex*.
It's not love, I know that. I've loved lots of women. And
once ignited, love rarely ever dies, so I never *stopped* loving
them. But I *did* stop *fucking* them (or being fucked *by* them,
rather, as I'm a lazy bottom).

Monogamy—not just in marriage but in cohabitations
of any length of time—is an unnatural state for human
beings. We're genetically programmed in the strands of our
DNA to fuck as many different people as we can to produce
as many offspring as we can so as to keep the species going.
In this, we're no different from the animals that terrify us or
taste delicious: Remove the lofty ambitions, and we're here
to fuck and make more of us so that the human race never
goes the way of the dinosaurs, which now exist solely at the
summer box office.

That's why it's always impressive when people get married, or even just live monogamously with each other: It goes against biology. You're conquering everything your monkey brain is telling you to do by bedding down with only one person; you're telling nature to go fuck itself. Some folks can't quit smoking, but with almost no effort, they'll quit other cock or pussy for life and dedicate their naked time to solely one partner. And that mini miracle happens every day, but we never celebrate it because a church or a greeting card will have you believe it's called love. It's not; it's cum. Don't let anyone dress up cum and tell you it's love. We love many, we cum with few.

And the first time I came with Jennifer Schwalbach was during unprotected sex while sporting an open wound on my dick.

Jennifer eventually tested me on the message board at Viewaskew.com, posting an entreaty to e-mail her. I wrote back instantly asking for her phone number. We'd just finished another round of *Dogma* rehearsals when I called Jennifer from my hotel room at the Westin William Penn in Pittsburgh.

"See?" I asked. "I told you I'd be watching. Mother Sister always watches."

She didn't catch the *Do the Right Thing* reference, but I didn't care because this wasn't Bryan Johnson or Scott Mosier, or someone with whom I'd share the language of pop culture; this was Jennifer Schwalbach—the young woman with that amazing job at *USA Today*. Her piece hadn't run yet, but she said her bosses dug what she was writing so much, they were giving her more space for the article. We talked for two hours, making a sorta date to talk again the next night.

All that morning, I was listening to famous movie stars read aloud words *I'd* written. Damon, Affleck, Rickman, Hayek, Rock, Lee, Fiorentino, Mewes—I barely heard any of them that day. All I could think about was Schwalbach and our phone date for that night. What would we talk about? How long would the conversation last *this* time? Was it at all possible that this chick might actually *like* me? I mean *like me* like me?

That night, we talked for four hours. I got maybe one hundred and twenty minutes of sleep before waking and directing stunt-Rock Derrick Simmons's fall from the sky. The next night, we talked again. Always deep, always fun, always informative. The *Dogma* shoot is a blur to me, but those nightly getting-to-know-you marathons with Jen are crystal clear. It's not hard to forget, as she's still very much that same fascinating, pussy-carrying puzzle to me that she was over a Pittsburgh phone line, more than a decade ago.

Once again, like Zeus at his chessboard, Gina Gardini would change my fate by throwing me into another room with Jennifer Schwalbach. This time, however, it wouldn't be a hotel room.

The Independent Spirit Awards were being held in a giant tent on the beach in Santa Monica, and *Chasing Amy* had gotten a fistful of nominations. But I was knee-deep in *Dogma* rehearsals and not interested in flying across the country to lose to Robert Duvall for *The Apostle*, so I'd passed. That's when Gina called.

"The IFP is urging us to send a representative for

Amy—which usually means the film's going to win something. They strongly suggested sending you. And Harvey says you've gotta go."

"When?"

"Saturday," Gina told me. "You leave Pittsburgh early in the morning and you're on a flight home from L.A. that night."

"Less than twenty-four hours," I confirmed, a genuine, giant non-L.A. fan. "Or I'm not going."

I called Jen, who'd been covering the awards circuit for *USA Today* that year, hitting the Oscars, the Golden Globes, and even the Blockbuster Awards. Since she was all over the awards spectrum, I asked her if she was doing the Indie Spirit Awards as well.

"I'm not," she replied.

"Damn . . ." I sighed.

"Why?"

"Well, I'm flying out for the Spirits, but I don't know anybody in Los Angeles anymore," I lied. "And since you were doing all the award shows for the paper, I thought maybe you'd be at this one, too, so at least there was someone in the tent I might kinda know."

"Do you want me to go with you to the Spirit Awards?" She made the heavy lifting easier. I quickly followed up with the fat-guy assurance.

"It wouldn't be a date-date," I said, even though it *would* be a date-date. "It's just being there together—but only because I thought you were already going."

"I'll go," she declared, sounding like Diane Court. And I, her very plump Lloyd Dobler, hung up the phone, called Salma Hayek, and let her know I wouldn't be her chaste-date for the Indie Spirit Awards as previously arranged. I told Salma Hayek that I had a serious shot at pussy far above my pay grade. I'm sure she was just glad I wasn't talking about *her* pussy, so she told me to chase it.

I left on the earliest flight out of Pittsburgh on a Saturday morning, which got me into LAX an hour before the show. I grabbed my bag and cabbed it to the Santa Monica beach, just as the red carpet was emptying and folks were getting seated for the show inside. I looked for Jen for a few seconds before she emerged from the tent, dressed to thrill. She was quite simply *stunning* and very out of my league. Thankfully, I was at the thinnest I'd ever been in my adult life: 230 pounds. I'd borrowed a Versace jacket from wardrobe that I was wearing atop a Graphitti Designs Superman logo T-shirt and jeans (full pants, not shorts), so I actually looked presentable as well. Jen took my arm and led me to the Miramax table, where Harvey leaned over and asked me, "Who's this?"

"A journalist," I whispered back. Harvey shot me a very disapproving look and clammed up for the remainder of the evening—most of which I wasn't around for anyway.

When the Best Screenplay winner was announced, as if God was trying to help me win this fine woman's heart, my dick lily was gilded with a golden statue. I got up and gave a funny acceptance speech, playing to the whole room but putting on my absolute best performance for an audience of *one*. After the thank-you speech, I was whisked backstage to do press, returning to the podium to give away an award and also joining Jason Lee to hug him onstage while he received *his* award as Best Supporting Actor for *Chasing Amy*. But from the moment I got up from the Miramax table, I never sat back down that entire day. In fact, by the time I'd emerged from backstage after doing all the press requests Miramax lined up, Jennifer was one of the only people left in the tent. I apologized for abandoning her, but she said she'd forgive me so long as we fucking *left* already. We climbed into her fire-engine-red Jeep, the Cherry Bomb, and hit the 10 East.

"Where do you wanna go?" she asked, all long hair and sunglasses in the blinding California sun. I wanted to say, "Anywhere you're going . . . ," but instead managed to spit out, "Your place."

"Oh, no," she said, slowing the car, offering me wide eyes. "My place is a pigsty."

"I don't care. I just wanna change out of these nice clothes and put on a hoodie."

She looked at my clothes, which really weren't all that nice, and asked, "You can't just do that in the car?"

"We're in and out," I promised.

Soon, we were at Jen's single-girl apartment on Poinsettia. She warned me again about the mess I was about to see before letting me into the least messy apartment I'd ever laid eyes on. I got changed and left my luggage and laptop locked in her bedroom as we took off to grab some eats. And for the next two glorious hours at Jerry's Famous Deli, I sat across from Jennifer Schwalbach and gazed into her eyes, watching her lips move as she spoke. Mind you, this was only the second time we'd ever even been in each other's company, with most of our courting having been done via e-mail and on the phone. So as pretty as I thought she was *before* I knew much about her, the details made her truly *dazzling*. March 23, 1998, is not only the date of my favorite meal at Jerry's Famous Deli, it's also the date of my favorite meal I've ever eaten. And while the food tasted better because I was falling in love, it was Jen Schwalbach's company that made that dinner what it was for me: the first in what I hoped would be a long line of shared suppers with the most interesting person I'd ever met.

After dinner, we walked around her neighborhood talking, killing time before I had to head back to LAX for a flight back to Pittsburgh. Eventually, we went back to her apartment, where she wouldn't show me her driver's license and I wouldn't show her my Mad Hatter tattoo. She suggested a swap, but I drove a harder bargain: I'd show her the tat if I could touch her ears.

It sounds creepy now, but in the moment, it was chaste and sweet. Jen's got these big-ass, Dumbo-looking ears that will allure the *fuck* out of an ear man like myself when they poke out from the midst of long, girly hair. This was my big move: I wanted to touch her ears before I flew back to Pittsburgh. Luckily, Schwalbach's a modern woman: Suddenly, she had her head in my lap, face up, saying, "Okay: touch my ears."

Meanwhile, even at my adult thinnest, I was still sucking in the gut. A fat man *always* has his gut sucked in—even when a gorgeous woman has her head in his lap. *Especially* when a gorgeous woman has her head in his lap. So here was this girl I was nuts about, head facing up in my lap, and I was unable to breathe, not because I was in love . . . but because if I exhaled, I ran the risk of releasing a flab-alanche that would certainly suffocate the poor girl, if not knock her head off my lap entirely.

And the whole time we were talking, I was trying to

discern whether she was into me or was just being polite since I was a guest in her home. The head in the lap wasn't clue enough for me because I'm a retarded jackass with zero self-confidence. I wanted to kiss her, but what if she did the duck? What if she got weirded out and it registered on her face? What if I went to kiss her and she vomited upward, at my face?

There was this old Graphitti Designs Flaming Carrot T-shirt Walt Flanagan always used to wear whenever we'd go comics hunting or play street hockey on the tennis courts. Worn to perfection, it featured Bob Burden's indie comic sensation swinging from a rope with a girl in his arms, emblazoned with the logo *Fortune Favors the Bold!* I decided to test the wisdom of that T-shirt. Tossing caution and fear to the wind, I leaned down and gently mashed my lips against Jennifer Schwalbach's. Much to my delight, she didn't retreat in the least; she kissed *back.*

That kiss led to an hour-long make-out session on her couch, which included some rigorous, desperate jeans-on-jeans dry-humping. An hour in, she asked me about the flight I was supposed to be on that night. I told her I'd rather stay in L.A. and talk to her all night, insisting I'd sleep on the couch. In the most seductive and promising whisper, Jennifer said I didn't have to sleep on the couch, then hopped up playfully and excused herself, shutting her bedroom door.

Alone finally after nearly thirty minutes of grueling groin pain, I unzipped my jeans to discover all the dry-humping Jen and I were doing had left a mark: a Potter-ish jagged scar that was, unfortunately, on the wrong head. The grinding we'd been doing on the couch was so intense that

Jen had ground the zipper of my jeans right through my underwear, into my very tender dickhead. There was a cut, some blood, and the looming prospect of an abrupt ending to what was easily the best night of my life. I zipped up just as Jennifer emerged from her bedroom, dressed in a nightie that didn't scream sex but also didn't communicate hand job either. The room behind her was full of lit candles. The message was clear. The dick pain, however, was excruciating.

We hit the bed and went back to making out. She got my pants off, but I was hoping I could spend so much time eating her pussy, she wouldn't go for my cock. I hoped maybe she'd be so tuckered and sated after I'd eaten at the Y for an hour that she'd just roll over and go to sleep, leaving my injured little soldier for the MASH helicopter to take away. From what I'd seen, the fucker'd been damn near decapitated; the last thing it needed was sexual attention, or any other attention for that matter.

But Schwalbach was going for the gusto. If this was to be a one-night stand, she was gonna get what she wanted, and that was a good fuckin'. Even *without* the wiener slitzel, however, she was never gonna be getting that from the likes of *me*. Had she known she was in hot pursuit of a bloody, battered dick, she might've changed her mind. Hell, had she realized all a fat man's gonna offer in bed is the Snoopy's Doghouse (he lies down, someone climbs on top of him, and he *gets* fucked), she likely would've run screaming from her own apartment. That position over and over can get boring, as my wife will tell you, but it's chiefly a precautionary measure: You do *not* want someone of my girth and width losing balance due to poor upper-body strength and collapsing on you. Even with all the cushiony blubber, an impact like that can take out a rib or flatten a boob worse than a mammogram.

So in the midst of all this carnality, there finally came a moment of truth, when it was clear the pussy could be licked no more and the time for cock lodgin' was at hand. I made one last-ditch effort to get out of fucking without hurting her feelings or further hurting my dick.

"I don't have protection," I said, not lying.

"You don't need it," was her response as she reached down to guide my cock into her body, her thumb resting on and *in* the dry-humping Potter-ish scar. When she slid that bolt home, I was in agony and ecstasy at the same time. It hurt so good, I thought Pinhead and the chattering-teeth Cenobite were gonna show up and tear my soul apart. After all, hell awaits the piece of shit who has unprotected sex while sporting an open wound! I knew the right thing to do was to fess up and tell her what all that dry-humping had done to my playmaker. I should've told her we needed to wait 'til I healed—because you're never supposed to have condomless sex with a stranger while sporting an open wound. Instead, I kept schtum and rode to glory.

It was the most irresponsible and risky thing I ever did, sinking my cut-open cock into Schwalbach's nethers—and I paid for it dearly. Being enveloped by those soaking lips should've felt like heaven on earth, but instead, it felt like I'd stuck my dick in battery acid. It burned with the heat of a thousand suns, and in my mind's eye, I could see my dick melting like it was a Nazi opening the Lost Ark. But I never let on; instead, I simply had the best and most painful sex of my life that night.

Doesn't that sound *horrible*? It's everything they taught

us *not* to do in the age of AIDS awareness and *dangerously* irresponsible. And yet, I married the girl, we had a daughter, and thus far, we've lived happily ever after. There's some more tough shit right there: Sometimes, you've gotta throw caution to the wind to find the treasure. Human beings do some stupid shit in an effort to cum with assistance: We *hate* to cum by ourselves. I speak for my gender when I say guys beat the truth out of their cocks regularly, often multiple times a day (sometimes more than once in a sitting), but like Heimdall at the gates of Asgard, it's something we do more dutifully than happily. We're lazy when it comes to ejaculating, so we're always looking for a hand. Or a mouth. Or a vagina.

Or a *leg*.

Cut to nearly a decade later: Jen was getting ready to go out one night, and as she stood in the bathroom mirror in nothing but a towel, she suddenly became fascinating to me, the most interesting person not only in the world, but especially in the room at that moment. And to top it off, there was easy access to crown jewels usually encased in grope-proof pajamas or tight jeans that porky paws can never breach.

So I joined her at the bathroom mirror and started laying on hands like a tent-revival preacher, as if I could exorcise whatever demon she was housing . . . so *I* could move in instead. Now, the wife's eight kinds of clever, so she can smell the hustle coming from miles away. Suddenly Mr. Twitter has shut his laptop and come a-courting. In response, still applying her war paint, Jen started closures of her own, locking those legs at the knees.

I started tugging at her towel in an effort to disappoint

this captivating creature one more time. All the blood that normally fuels common sense had now rushed to a cock so rigid and unbreakable, I could have cut diamonds with it. I looked down and saw the tip of the head poking out from under my belly—a rarity for this zaftig boy. And as I mounted up yet again for a ride inside my bride, Jennifer backed me off with the most powerful sentiment a wife can impart to her husband of ten years, the sharer of her dreams, adventures, and hopes, and father of her only begotten daughter . . .

"I don't want you leaking out of me all night."

This would be a major wrinkle in the campaign of most men, but as a married man, I knew this meant we were merely negotiating. I presented my counteroffer.

"Head?"

"It's not your birthday . . . ," she muttered, applying her lipstick as if it were a Rubicon I dared not cross.

"Can you jerk me off?"

"Jerk *yourself* off."

"Now we're getting somewhere," I thought. And that's when I heard these sad, desperate words leap from my lips . . .

"Well, can I at least look at your asshole while I jerk off?"

Most women would have been repulsed, but Schwalbach has had *years* to get used to the sad mess that is the man she married. Many a night, she's had to pull open a pity cheek in the bed for the chatty fatty who wants to play looksies. She gently sighs each time I remind her that it was always my dream as a twelve-year-old tubster to look at a naked lady whenever I wanted. Had I known there'd be an Internet one day, perhaps I wouldn't have romanticized marriage so. But

since I came (and came, and came . . .) of age in a more innocent time, I'm sentimental about marriage and a big believer in the institution, defined in the great Garden State of
New Jersey as a legal union in which both partners are con-
tractually forced to share nudity and orgasms with each
other.

So with all the patience of a Canadian saint, Jen stepped
her legs apart slightly as the towel dropped. And while she
continued to put on her face in the bathroom mirror, my
wife-for-life announced, "You've got five minutes."

Gentle reader, I needed merely one minute before I can-
noned millions of potential Harley siblings into the back of
my wife's knee. That's the beauty of marriage: You bind
yourself to someone who understands that every once in a
while, you've gotta chimp out and answer to that primal
teenager still buried in your brain who wants to explore and
do all the weird shit you'd fantasized about while pounding
pudd back home at Mom and Dad's. Sometimes, in order for
a marriage to work, you've gotta let your spouse stare at
your asshole and jerk off while you're busy doing something else. No Catholic priest is ever gonna tell you that in a
Pre-Cana Conference; that comes from a soldier who's spent
the past dozen years in the trenches . . . or rather, *Jen's* trench—
which I'm using metaphorically, of course, and not as de-
scriptive of the length, depth, or width of her hoo-ha.

Faced with the dismal prospect of cumming alone, even
the mighty fall to their knees—in this case, literally. Picture,
if you will, a beautiful, tall, dignified, naked woman primp-
ing in the bathroom mirror as Jabba the Hutt kneels at her
backside like she's a rack of candles in church, tugging one
out while he spectates before her anus.

And that, my friends, is the very definition of *marriage*. In marriage, we walk through life with a partner—someone you never have to be afraid of saying dopey, depraved shit in front of. Rather than run screaming, Schwalbach weighed a certainty against a doubt, dropped her towel, and let me perv out, literally behind her back. Jen Schwalbach was and continues to be my favorite person in the world because I've never had more fun with any other living creature than I have with her. That's not just a wife, that's a *dream girl*.

Achieving your dreams isn't hard. Like anything in life, there's an equation to follow: You've gotta learn how to dream practically wild while conducting yourself as wildly practical. I didn't dream of curing cancer or traveling to another galaxy for a career; I chose something that seemed achievable: film. Other cats who didn't seem any more special than I was had made movies; why not *me*?

But while dreaming is free and fun, you've gotta make sure you manage your expectations. Accept that nothing will ever go for you exactly as it went for someone else, but more important, know that you never get *exactly* what you want; it's usually a modified or over-the-top version of what you sought in the first place. In my case, I wanted a career in the arts, so I could remain an adolescent my entire adult life.

But art is not math: The numbers don't always add up or make sense—which is part of art's magic. However, magic isn't a predictable construct; it's an alchemy you pray will work each time, not a de facto recipe for success. If you wanna be in film, creative writing, music, painting, or performance, know that there are very few concretes—because, chiefly, your job is to make believe. That's all "talented" adults really are: overgrown children, unwilling to accept standard-issue adulthood. If you feel the circus calling, answer her, but know that you may be in for a life of sacrifice to attain your goals. There is no financial security in any creative pursuit. If you want certainty, get out of art.

Just learn to manage your expectations. Be malleable—so that if all that's open to your square peg is a round hole, you can still make it work. Sometimes, you're so wrapped up in the details, you forget there is lots more to the picture. The canvas of art is vast; be happy you get to add any color to it, not bitchy about which crayons are taken. Shine with what you got.

I learned this by observing my wife for the last decade-plus. Jennifer managed *her* expectations when she hooked up with me. My wife's a good-looking woman and I'm a fat schlub. She could have done a lot better than me and landed one of those thin boys with roving eyes. But she knew that while she'd have to look past my perceived deficit of a spare-tire belly, I was above par in most other areas that counted: I was loyal, interesting, funny, a great provider, and I ate pussy like it contained the cure for fat, or more likely, sugar—the *source* of fat. Thin boys may not have the gut, but that means they also have more options, because *everybody* wants thin and in shape. But if you fuck a dude nobody wants to fuck—a fat dude—you can be relatively sure he'll never cheat on you. And even *better*? He'll show you insane appreciation for making the alternative choice—even over the course of a lifetime.

Jen managed her expectations, yes—but she also sacrificed. Film had taken over my life years before I met Jen. Since 1991, making movies was the prime directive: It was my passion, my art, all I wanted to do in life, and yet it never seemed impossible to accomplish. Richard Linklater had done it with *Slacker*. Hal Hartley had done it with *The Unbelievable Truth* and *Trust*. Spike Lee had broken through with *She's Gotta Have It*. P. J. Castellaneta shot the gay film *Together Alone* for less than ten grand, while Robert Rodriguez made an entire action movie allegedly for seven thousand dollars. None of these guys seemed anointed by God, unless you consider Harvey Weinstein the Almighty; why, then, couldn't *I* do it as well?

By the time I'd met Jen Schwalbach, I'd committed my life to film, much in the same way the clergy commit their lives to Christ. But Jesus requires a leap of faith in *Him*; film would require a leap of faith in *me*. Making movies was all I wanted to do, so I organized my life around cinema. If folks wanted to share time with me or be in my world, they had to understand that film would always be my first love.

When I met Jen, I was in pre-production on *Dogma* and well established in the indie film pantheon as the guy who shot onto the scene with *Clerks*, stumbled at the box office with *Mallrats*, and took a huge jump with the truly indie *Chasing Amy*—a film about male sexual insecurity and the nature of love. I'd soared and sunk and come back from the brink of irrelevancy, going from overnight sensation to indie whipping boy to drunken master—a cycle that would repeat every few years for the rest of my life in film. I was *entrenched* in movies and *nothing* was gonna get me out of them.

Jennifer Schwalbach was a journalist at the biggest newspaper in the world. She'd just gotten her own byline when we were thrown together for the *Good Will Hunting* spinterview. She was going places . . . until we fell in love. And in order to give us half a shot at making it as a couple, Jennifer made the most noble and unthinkable sacrifice for the greater good. She quit her job.

In fact, Jen quit *two* jobs for me and my world. First, she left *USA Today*, moving east to be closer to me. She'd landed a gig at MTV in New York City and was making excellent progress when the Kevin Smith Effect would knock her even further off her own path: Jen got pregnant with Harley. Soon, the MTV gig would be sacrificed at the altar of our relationship—the altar she built and maintained because I was too busy making dopey movies back in Jersey. Just like me, Jennifer Schwalbach had ambitions and dreams of accomplishments that would make her parents proud. Unlike me, Jennifer Schwalbach was willing to chuck it all for something profoundly more rewarding.

That's some tough shit right there: knowing you destroyed the life of the only person you'd take a bullet for. Jenny Schwalbach's potential was hampered and hindered because she fell in love with the wrong guy—one of those fucking filmmakers who thinks solely about himself and his work, who plays for a living and makes pretend for money. The portrait of the artist as a young man slowly devolves into the depiction of a self-involved paid liar with a half-lived life—more make-believe than reality. I would have been alone in that life—perhaps lost in my art eventually—because film is a siren that calls you to her jagged rocks to pick your bones clean, then lies in wait for another hapless dreamer to sail by. You give yourself to something old and massive that promises immortality but instead uses you up and moves on. But we don't ever bitch: The life of an artist is vibrant, electric, and fulfilling . . . until it's not anymore. And after decades spent pursuing something with all the passion and purpose of Odysseus, to paraphrase *Conan the Barbarian*'s King Osric, "There comes a time, thief, when the jewels cease to sparkle, when the gold loses its luster, when the throne room becomes a prison, and all that is left is a guy's love for the chick he initially believed was a hooker paid for by Chris Rock."

For years, I thought I was doing the important work, but movies are just smoke and mirrors and shadows and fog. Telling the lie that tells the truth doesn't take courage so much as it takes a willingness to lay down your life in service of making shit up. In that, it's no different from child's play: Filmmakers fill their time with empty celluloid distractions, maintaining each is an important pursuit with all the passion and vehemence kids display when *they* frolic in lands of make-believe on a playground, in a schoolyard, or in their bedrooms. It's the epic diversion from the all-encompassing truth that one day very soon, we will cease to be.

In the time since I met Jennifer Schwalbach, I made some dippy flicks a few people liked. In the same time, however, Jennifer did so much more: She built a life with a family she's personally responsible for bringing together. She built a home for the people she loves most dearly in this world, where they can feel safe, dream their dreams, and be productive. And most important, Jen built and maintains an entire *human being*.

Like most kids her age, Harley's a dreamer. What sets her apart, however, is that she takes her dreams to fruition. Some leaders display the kinds of take-charge qualities that are more easily identifiable, but the leaders like Harley—

whose passion is infectious enough to create something out of nothing—lead by inspiration. And behind all the passion beats the heart of a true humanist . . . as well as a humorist: She's funny—and not in that cloying manner like some kids can be. Her humor's warm, inclusive, and friendly. In that respect, Harley's who I'd most like to be when I grow up.

And that was all Jen. I donated a teaspoon full of what was hopefully the best parts of me, but Jen knew that in order to make a whole person, more time needed to be donated than the five minutes it might've taken me to muster the building blocks of Harley. Jen knew it was going to take sacrifice, and since my head was way up my own ass about movies, she knew in order to will this family into existence, *she'd* have to be the one to give things up, and maybe even give herself *entirely*.

We've been together fourteen years now, and my passion has shifted from film to family. After years of making shit up, now I'm entranced by the cold hard reality of it all, the wonder of the mundane and average; the blurred line between life and diversion doesn't require made-up people and situations anymore, and the investment in recording simple conversation is about time, not dimes. When we launched *Plus One*, I got to combine my love of podcasting and my love of talking to (and making fun of) Jen. Sometimes, we're even joined by Harley, so I get to incorporate my entire family in my art—which is only fitting, as I've been my wife's art project for over a decade now and my kid is gonna have to dwell on this earth for all time as Silent Bob's daughter. Now I'm more interested in capturing their feelings, thoughts, ideas, and chatter. Motherfuck make-pretend characters in a ninety-minute stoner comedy; gimme real, interesting people with a point of view. And as far as I'm concerned, I'm surrounded by *real*, interesting people. Now it's *their* time to take center stage—whether they're public people or not.

And I know all the podcasts in paradise will never make up for the life Jennifer gave up in order to join my traveling sideshow, even if she did promptly make it her own. It's a debt that humbles me, and one I can never repay in full. We can accomplish very little by ourselves in this world, so we look to others to help us flesh out our whimsies. And every once in a while, a player so great comes along, they improve *your* game. I've achieved a lot of my goals, but usually because someone was there to feed me a pass I could one-time into twine.

One of my favorite aspects of the Gretzky mythos is his insane stats that dominate every other top athlete in their respective sports by massive margins. When he retired from the game, Gretzky had 894 regular-season goals—a jaw-dropper of a number. But the *real* story is told in his *assists* record: 1,963. Nearly two thousand times, the greatest hockey player who ever lived passed the puck to someone else to put in the net. That's more than *double* the amount of times he took the shot *himself.* Instead of trying to grab the glory, he shared the wealth and elevated *others.* Gretzky was a team player with an astounding work ethic and an uncanny ability to see not only where the game was, but where the game was eventually *going*—and rather than keep that light under a bushel, he spread it around, using it to illuminate the talents of others. There is nothing more beautiful in hockey or in that excellent metaphor for hockey

called life than the assist: You give of yourself so that someone else can achieve *their* goal.

Jen has been my Gretzky for years now. She regularly
feeds me passes and elevates my game. I score and win because I've got an unselfish, talented teammate who feels it's
better to give than receive and believes it's better to assist
than score. And on top of that, she's got one up on Gretzky:
She fucks me. And being fucked by Jennifer Schwalbach is
my idea of heaven, because she can fuck like a demon.

If life had anything like the Hockey Hall of Fame, Jen
Schwalbach would be inducted into the Builder category.
And under her plaque, it'd say, "Jennifer Schwalbach always
seemed to know where the puck was going but used that
talent to help others reach *their* goals instead—particularly
an anonymous, untalented fat boy from New Jersey who
fell in love with her hard. Without a doubt, she truly is the
Great One."

Taking Someone Else's Shit

How'd I learn all this shit, anyway? I'd like to credit my years of experience, but I'm only forty-one *chronologically*, and I haven't acted my age in decades. No, I learned how to deal with most of what I know *before* it even happened to me because I watched someone else lead by example and studied *their* work.

I've always looked at John Hughes—the legendary writer/director who gave us *Sixteen Candles* and *The Breakfast Club*—as the filmmaker I most related to, even though I never met him. Hughes made movies about my generation when nobody else seemed to give a shit. While similar movies reduced young people to cum-crazy fuck machines, Hughes portrayed teens as human beings with slightly less experience than their elders, but no less self-awareness. The people in his flicks resembled the people you knew in real life, the dialogue was always did-you-secretly-record-me-and-my-friends-or-something perfect, reflecting the thoughts, fears, chuckles, and dreams of teenagers in the '80s.

The mark of any classic piece of filmmaking is longevity, and the Hughes oeuvre holds up thirty years later. John Hughes may have died, but while you can't still see the man, you can hear him, feel him, and maybe even know him a little bit thanks to his life's work in cinema. He remains beloved because Hughes was the first one of *us*—the movie geeks, the loners, the glasses-wearers, the Farmer Teds—to make it *inside* the dream factory, where he told *his* stories (which also happened to be *our* stories as well).

But a writer rarely works on one level only. If wordsmiths are magicians who fill your head with incantations and magical spells, John Hughes was a sorcerer supreme: the storyteller not content to give you what you wanted to see and hear, but also eager to tell you what you needed to know about life, and warn you of the tough shit to come.

Ferris Bueller's Day Off is John Hughes's classic piece of proto-slacker cinema. We've all thought about ditching for the day at one point or another in our scholastic careers (and likely from our jobs as adults, too), and we've all watched as Matthew Broderick bent the rules in pursuit of a little me-time. But while Hughes chiefly wanted to entertain us, I've always felt he used *Ferris* to do *more* than tell his *or* our tale; I think he used his flick to send a message to all the geeks who'd follow: *"I've cracked the code."*

In *Ferris*, Hughes was trying to communicate simple tenets that, when followed, would offer the happiest, most carefree existence people like *us* could ever require. And by *us* I mean the Breakfast Clubbers. The Weird Scientists. The Pretties in Pink. Generation Hughes, if you will.

I always appreciated the fact that John Hughes somehow made my life a little easier with his words. Hopefully, that's what *Tough Sh*t* has done for you, dearly beloved, gentle reader. However, if in this tome I've thus far failed to provide you with a single useful sentiment or a decent enough road map to help get you through this thing called life, let me point you to *my* sensei. I've always been but a Padawan Youngling; the late, great Master Hughes was the *true* Jedi. And like an old Jedi in the sand dunes, he bestowed upon the Luke Skywalker of our collective consciousness the gift of not only a faith we could believe in, but also one fucker of a lightsaber: Buellerism.

THE TENETS OF BUELLERISM

- Get along with everyone. Strive to be welcomed by all: sportos, motorheads, geeks, sluts, bloods, wastoids, dweebies, dickheads. Be a righteous dude.

- Look out that window. How can you possibly be expected to handle school/work/insert-worry-here on a day like this?

- Your parents are clueless, but they love you. And the key to faking them out is the clammy hands.

- Lay off your brother; he loves you.

- Your sister loves you, but she also knows you're full of shit.

- It is no problem whatsoever to always provide all pertinent information on any given subject.

- Stay cool. Remember: When the meek get pinched, the bold survive.

- Never condone fascism, or any -ism for that matter. Quote John Lennon often, as he knew what he was talking about: He was the Walrus who never had to bum rides off people.

- Never say no to a limo—particularly a nice stretch job with a TV and a bar.

- Distrust authority or anyone who has a problem with a little bending of the rules. Only rules you gotta follow are the ones that keep you out of the police station. Otherwise you'll end up like Charlie Sheen. Sorry—Charlie Sheen's character.

- Gordie Howe was number 9 on the Detroit Red Wings.

- Hide in plain sight. Lip-synch in the face of danger.

- Always park your own car.

- Always lock the garage. And running a car in reverse doesn't turn the mileage back.

- Take some time for yourself every once in a while. At least nine times a year.

- If people don't like your policies, they can smooch your big ol' white (or other shade) butt. Pucker up, Buttercup.

- Play only by the rules if you enjoy gym.

- In any game where the score is zero-zero, there's always a winner: the Bears.

- A fifth-grade threat still packs an amazing amount of influence.

- Between grief and nothing, take grief.

- The Smoot-Hawley Tariff Act raised tariffs in an effort to collect more revenue for the federal government. This was akin to something–d-o-o economics. "Voodoo" economics.

- You can't respect somebody who kisses your ass. It just doesn't work.

- Stay in bed when you're ill; in your weakened condition, you could take a nasty spill down the stairs and subject yourself to further school absences.

- The word *asshole* is French.

- Don't go to college all wound up so tight, or your roommate will kill you.

- Don't let the snooty or the snotty stand in the way of a good time. Let 'em know who you are: Abe Froman—the Sausage King of Chicago.

- Youth will always leave the cheese of the old out in the wind.

- You can never go too far. But if you're gonna get busted, don't let it be by a guy like that.

- Don't live your life like you're in some kind of museum that's very beautiful and very cold, where you're not allowed to touch anything.

- Swing, batta.

- *Les jeux sont faits!*

- Life moves pretty fast. If you don't stop and look around once in a while, you could miss it.

A Little Shit for the Road

So here's the tough shit about *Tough Sh*t* . . .

This book is not a blueprint: It's just some funny and bittersweet stuff that happened to me that I feel shaped me into a more well-rounded person—so round, in fact, that a major airline gave me shit about it. But *Tough Sh*t* is not the Necronomicon. It will not raise the dead.

But it might have an effect on the *living*.

If you're alive, kick into drive. Chase whimsies. See if you can turn dreams into a way to make a living, if not an entire way of life. Sure, *skill* will take you far in this world, but we're not all blessed with natural ability. I'm proud to be living proof that even if you're a talentless boob from the Jersey burbs, *will* can take you just as far.

But always remember, kids: I'm as full of shit as the next guy. Not in a maliciously misleading way: I'm just a flawed-ass human being like everyone else, so what do I know? Take this entire book with a pound of salt: I may write about how my dad died screaming, yet I'm still the asshole that doesn't call or see his mother nearly enough.

And I may talk about not giving a shit about what critics have to say . . . but yet, there was one review of my stuff this year that I not only read *multiple* times, the review actually made me cry.

As a Christmas gift, my daughter, Harley, wrote an essay about me—an overview not of *filmmaker* Kevin Smith, but Kevin Smith the *dad*. Considering it's the best review I've ever gotten, I'm including it here, for posterity.

I hope she still feels the same way when she's a teenager . . .

> *Usually a Father is seen as an authority figure that is just there to keep you in line. That's not how I see my dad at all.*
>
> *To me my dad is my role model. Without my dad I don't know what I'd do. A lot of people say we are just a like and I think so as well.*
>
> *I can't relate anyone as much as him. No one really understands what I'm feeling sometimes except for my dad. When I'm sad, a lot of people will just tell me to brush it off and get through the day, but my dad will relate to me. He always tells me something that makes me feel better or how to get through my problem. When I am feeling really sensitive he is the only one that can really understand how I'm feeling.*
>
> *My dad is my role model in so many ways. I see him go through a lot of things sometimes, and he*

always knows how to get through them. He doesn't really care what anyone thinks and he is himself. Like for instance one day he told me about some of the mean stuff people say on Twitter and I didn't really understand how that couldn't hurt his feelings and he said that you couldn't please everyone. I really admire that because sometimes I try to go out of my way to make someone happy by not being my self, but he is always himself and everyone loves him for that. He is very inspiring and always has quotes handy to give when I'm feeling down.

My dad helped me find out what I love to do most in life, which is making people laugh. I can't always get a laugh out of everyone, but when I do it makes me feel really happy and my dad helped me figure that out being the hilarious person that he is. I used to be sad when I made people laugh because I thought they were laughing at me, but now I know that making people laugh is the best feeling in the whole world.

My dad is very kind hearted and always has an open ear for me to talk to him. Sometimes no one really understands my ideas or understands why I like something but he will understand. Without my dad I would not like to write as much as I probably do. A lot of the time when I am either really sad or really happy my dad will tell me to write and put my emotions into the writing and that I can let it all out there. My dad encourages me to write all the time and I really appreciate that because before I found writing as just something I had to do for school, but now I really like writing and I do it for fun.

Whenever I try something new my dad always makes me feel good about it. Like when I did the play I didn't really know how I was going to do, but then when I did it and my dad saw it he made me feel so good because he went on about how good I did.

My dad is always there for me even when he is miles and miles away I always think of him when I need a little inspiration or a little kick to get me going because I know he loves me and I love him just as much.

My dad is one of the most special people in my life and I do not know where I would be in life if he were any different then he is now.

I love my daddy.

—Harley Quinn Smith
12/25/11

Thanks and Shit!

I couldn't do any of the fun shit were it not for a steady stream of people who make my life possible.

Thanks to my mom, Grace Smith, for not only making me, but also making me who I am.

Thanks to my second mom, Gail Stanley, who kept my life, house, and family in order for ten years while I did lots of the stuff you read about in this book.

Thanks to Byron for being the finest surrogate dad Harley could ever have, and modestly taking no credit.

Thanks to my brother, Don, who always had cash to give me whenever I was broke, laughs for me when nobody else knew I was funny, and who always puts everyone else first.

Thanks to Reyna, who cleans my clothes, washes my dishes, and sometimes has to pick up the dog crap.

Thanks to Harley for *getting* me—and for never giving me any of that "Cat's in the Cradle" shit.

Thanks, of course, to the band of believers who help me make my dreams come true every week . . .

—My right arm, Meghan Quinlan—the tiny tornado.

50 KEVIN SMITH

—My left nut, Jason Mewes—the king of Why Not.

—My Hobson, Carol Hammond.

—My muscle, Jordan Monsanto.

—Meghan's right arm, Alan Wysocki.

—The penis to my sandwich, Ralph Garman.

—The only guy who could get *Red State* made, Jon Gordon.

—The slot machine that just keeps paying out, Elyse Seiden.

—Ming, who somehow finds time to do everything I ask for online.

—Jeff Hyman and Degy, for telling people I give oral.

—Our *Red State* investors in New York City and in Canada (NVSH).

—The entire S.I.R. and SModCo family.

But when it comes to the biggest thanks, it goes to the truest of believers. There is no better Sancho Panza in this world than my longtime crush and for-all-time partner, Jenny Schwalbach. She not only lets me do whatever I want with her body, she enables me to do whatever I want with my *life*.

And lastly, thanks to *you* guys—the audience. You continue to support everything SModCo does—be it movies, TV, podcasts, live shows or, as in the case of our latest whimsy-turned-reality, the movie "revue" show, SPOILERS (on Hulu in the U.S. and Space in Canada).

For posterity, what follows is a semicomplete list of all the screenings, live shows, podcasts, and general nonsense you allowed me to do—in just 2011 alone—by giving me your money and showing up to see or hear some SMod. Look at what *you* made happen . . .

JANUARY

12/31–1/1
Hollywood Babble-On New
  Years Fiasco
The Jon Lovitz Comedy
  Club and Podcast Theater,
  Universal CityWalk

1/1
Jay & Silent Bob Get Old
The Lovitz, Universal
  CityWalk

1/3
Red State of the Union: Kerry
  Bishe
SModcastle

1/7
8 P.M.: *Hollywood Babble-On*
10 P.M.: *Jay & Silent Bob Get
  Old*
The Lovitz, Universal CityWalk

1/10
Red State of the Union: Kyle
  Gallner
SModcastle

1/12
SModist at Nerdcastle Mash-Up
  Show
SModcastle

1/14
Jay & Silent Bob Get Old
The Lovitz, Universal CityWalk

1/15
Hollywood Babble-On
The Lovitz, Universal CityWalk

1/17
Red State of the Union: Michael
  Parks
SModcastle

1/18
AOL Late Night promo shoot
AOL, Los Angeles

1/23
Red State World Premiere
Sundance Film Festival
Park City, Utah

1/28
Jay & Silent Bob Get Old
The Lovitz, Universal CityWalk

1/29
Hollywood Babble-On
The Lovitz, Universal CityWalk

1/31
Kev on *Chelsea Lately*,
Los Angeles

FEBRUARY

2/4
Jay & Silent Bob Get Old
The Lovitz, Universal CityWalk

2/5
Hollywood Babble-On
The Lovitz, Universal CityWalk

2/7
Opie & Anthony
Sirius/XM, NYC
Gotham book deal for *Tough
  Sh*t*
Penguin Books, NYC

2/8
Imus in the Morning
NYC
Joy Behar Show
HLN, NYC

2/10
Red State International
    Distributor Screening
Berlin Film Festival Market,
    Germany

2/12
Hollywood Babble-On
The Lovitz, Universal CityWalk

2/13
Jay & Silent Bob Get Old
The Lovitz, Universal CityWalk

2/18
Real Time with Bill Mahr
Los Angeles
Jay & Silent Bob Get Old
The Lovitz, Universal CityWalk

2/19
Hollywood Babble-On
The Lovitz, Universal CityWalk

2/22
Piers Morgan
CNN, Los Angeles

2/23
Attack of the Show
G4TV, Los Angeles

2/23
Telepictures Meeting with Jim
    Paratore; *Tonitely* is born
Jen Schwalbach's House, Los
    Angeles

2/25
Hollywood Babble-On
The Lovitz, Universal CityWalk

2/26
Jay & Silent Bob Get Old
The Lovitz, Universal
    CityWalk

MARCH

3/4
Opie & Anthony
Sirius/XM, NYC
Midtown Comics Signing
NYC

3/5
Red State USA Tour
Screening/Q&A
Radio City Music Hall, NYC

3/6
Red State USA Tour
Screening/Q&A
Wilbur Theatre, Boston

3/8
Red State USA Tour
Screening/Q&A
Harris Theater, Chicago

3/9
Red State USA Tour
Screening/Q&A
State Theater, Minnesota

3/10
Red State USA Tour
Screening/Q&A
Michigan Theater, Ann Arbor

3/11
Red State USA Tour
Screening/Q&A
Clowes Hall, Indiana

3/12
Red State USA Tour
Screening/Q&A
Midland Theatre, Kansas City

3/14
Red State USA Tour
Screening/Q&A
Clark State, Ohio

3/15
Red State USA Tour
Screening/Q&A
Warner Theatre, Washington,
   D.C.

3/18
8 P.M.: *Jay & Silent Bob Get Old*
10 P.M.: *Hollywood Babble-On*
The Lovitz, Universal CityWalk

3/19
8 P.M.: *SModcast 3D*
10 P.M.: *Jay & Silent Bob Get Old*
Warfield Theater, San Francisco

3/22
Red State USA Tour
Screening/Q&A
Paramount Theatre, Denver

3/23
SModcast 3D
The Lovitz, Universal CityWalk

3/25
Jay & Silent Bob Get Old
The Lovitz, Universal CityWalk

3/26
Red State USA Tour
Screening/Q&A
AMC Theaters, New Orleans

3/28
Red State USA Tour
Screening/Q&A
Paramount Theatre, Austin

3/29
Red State USA Tour
Screening/Q&A
Cobb Center, Atlanta

3/30
8 P.M.: *SModcast 3D*
10 P.M.: *Jay & Silent Bob Get
   Old*
Hard Rock Live, Orlando

APRIL

4/1
8 P.M.: *SModcast 3D*
10 P.M.: *Jay & Silent Bob Get
   Old*
Carnegie Music Hall, Pittsburgh

4/2
Evening with Kevin Smith,
Keswick, Philadelphia

4/4
Red State USA Tour
Screening/Q&A
McCaw Hall, Seattle

4/8
8 P.M.: *Jay & Silent Bob Get Old*
10 P.M.: *Hollywood Babble-On*
The Lovitz, Universal CityWalk

4/9
Red State USA Tour Finale
Screening/Q&A
Wiltern Theater, Los Angeles

4/10
Kevin Smith Sells Out: The
    View Askew Garage Sale
Live Auction, Los Angeles

4/12
NAB Conference for AVID
Las Vegas

4/15
Allan Amato SModCo photo
    shoot
Jay & Silent Bob Get Old
The Lovitz, Universal
    CityWalk

4/16
Hollywood Babble-On
The Lovitz, Universal
    CityWalk

4/17
Red State at Quentin's
Tarantino's House, Los Angeles

4/22
Jay & Silent Bob Get Old
The Lovitz, Universal CityWalk

4/23
8 P.M.: *SModcast 3D*
10 P.M.: *Hollywood Babble-On*
The Lovitz, Universal
    CityWalk

4/29
Evening With Kevin Smith
Morristown, NJ

4/30
8 P.M.: *SModcast 3D*
10 P.M.: *Jay & Silent Bob Get
    Old*
Kingston, NY

MAY

5/2
8 P.M.: *SModcast 3D*
10 P.M.: *Jay & Silent Bob Get
    Old*
Midland Theatre, Kansas City

5/3
8 P.M.: *SModcast 3D*
10 P.M.: *Jay & Silent Bob Get
    Old*
Pabst Theater, Milwaukee

5/4
8 P.M.: *SModcast 3D*
10 P.M.: *Jay & Silent Bob Get
    Old*
Harris Theater, Chicago

5/6
Jay & Silent Bob Get Old
The Lovitz, Universal CityWalk

5/7
Hollywood Babble-On
The Lovitz, Universal CityWalk

5/9
S.I.R.! SModcast Internet Radio
    goes live
Jen Schwalbach's House, Los
    Angeles
*Cinema Enema w/ Jay & Silent
    Bob*
G4TV, Hollywood

5/11
Noel Biderman on *SMorning
    Show*
Jen Schwalbach's House, Los
    Angeles

5/13
Michael K Williams on
    SMorning Show
Jen Schwalbach's House, Los
    Angeles
Jay & Silent Bob Get Old
The Lovitz, Universal
    CityWalk

5/14
Hollywood Babble-On
The Lovitz, Universal
    CityWalk

5/17
*Cinema Enema w/ Jay & Silent
    Bob*
G4TV, Hollywood

5/18
Financial Times Interview/
    Photo
Jen Schwalbach's House, Los
    Angeles

5/19
Nick Braun on *SMorning Show*
Jen Schwalbach's House, Los
    Angeles

5/20
Jay & Silent Bob Get Old
The Lovitz, Universal CityWalk

5/21
Hollywood Babble-On
The Lovitz, Universal CityWalk

5/23
*Cinema Enema w/ Jay & Silent
    Bob*
G4TV, Hollywood

5/24
Marc Maron, Mick Foley on
    SMorning Show
Jen Schwalbach's House, Los
    Angeles
Jay & Silent Bob Get Old
The Lovitz, Universal CityWalk

5/26
Dan Etheridge on *SMorning
    Show*
Jen Schwalbach's House, Los
    Angeles

5/27
Scott Neidermayer on
    SMorning Show
Jen Schwalbach's House, Los
    Angeles
Jay & Silent Bob Get Old
The Lovitz, Universal CityWalk

5/28
Hollywood Babble-On
The Lovitz, Universal CityWalk

5/29
Poddammit—12-Hour Podcast
    Marathon
• *Babble-On* Comic-Con
    Theater
• *Let Us Act*
• *The ABCs of SNL*
• *Plus One Live*
• *Having Sex, with Katie
    Morgan*
The Lovitz, Universal CityWalk

5/31
Kurt Sutter and Katey Segal on
SMorning Show
Jen Schwalbach's House, Los
Angeles

JUNE

6/2
Julie Plec on *SMorning Show*
Jen Schwalbach's House, Los
Angeles

6/3
Jack Morrissey, Ethan Suplee on
SMorning Show
Jen Schwalbach's House, Los
Angeles
Jay & Silent Bob Get Old
The Lovitz, Universal CityWalk

6/4
Produced By Conference
Disney Lot, Burbank
Hollywood Babble-On
The Lovitz, Universal CityWalk

6/11
SMoviola: Valley Girl
Q&A with Martha Coolidge,
Deborah Foreman, Frederick
Elmes
Lincoln Center, NYC

6/12
AMC pilot shoot
Secret Stash, Red Bank

6/13–6/19
Red State at the Taor Mina Film
Fest
Meghan & Allan Get Engaged
Sicily, Italy

6/20
Joe Rogan on *SMorning Show*
Jen Schwalbach's House,
Los Angeles

6/21
SMoviola: Rocketeer
Q&A with Joe Johnston, Bill
Campbell, Danny Bilson,
Paul De Meo, Rick Baker,
William Stout
El Capitan Theater, Los Angeles

6/22
Deborah Foreman on *SMorning
Show*
Jen Schwalbach's House,
Los Angeles
NHL Awards
Norris Trophy Presenter
The Palms, Las Vegas

6/23
Marc Bernardin on *SMorning
Show*
Jen Schwalbach's House, Los
Angeles

6/24
Jay & Silent Bob Get Old
The Lovitz, Universal
CityWalk

6/25–6/26
Harley Birthday Weekend
Disneyland Hotel, Anaheim

6/27
Sara Benincasa on *SMorning
Show*
Jen Schwalbach's House, Los
Angeles

6/28
Nakia on *SMorning Show*
Jen Schwalbach's House,
    Los Angeles

6/29
Heidi Holiker, Ralph Garman
    on *SMorning Show*
Jen Schwalbach's House,
    Los Angeles
SModcastle Final Night/
    SModcastle Closes
SModcastle

JULY

7/1
Jensen Karp on *SMorning
    Show*
Jen Schwalbach's House, Los
    Angeles

7/2
Hollywood Babble-On
The Lovitz, Universal
    CityWalk

7/3
ABC's of SNL 2
The Lovitz, Universal
    CityWalk

7/5
Adam Brody on *SMorning
    Show*
Jen Schwalbach's House, Los
    Angeles

7/6
Jay Mohr on *SMorning Show*
Jen Schwalbach's House, Los
    Angeles

7/8
Zach Levi on *SMorning Show*
Jen Schwalbach's House,
    Los Angeles
8 P.M.: SMaudition
10 P.M.: *Hollywood Babble-On*
The Lovitz, Universal CityWalk

7/9
SMarriage
Gavin and Nikki
Jay & Silent Bob's Secret Stash,
    Red Bank

7/12
Christine Pazsitsky on
    SMorning Show
Jen Schwalbach's House,
    Los Angeles

7/13
Joe Utichi, Nikki Glaser on
    SMorning Show
Jen Schwalbach's House,
    Los Angeles

7/14
Chris Hardwick on *SMorning
    Show*
Jen Schwalbach's House,
    Los Angeles

7/15
Jay & Silent Bob Get Old
The Lovitz, Universal CityWalk

7/16
8 P.M.: SMarriage on S.I.R.
Melody and Mark
Jen Schwalbach's House,
    Los Angeles
10 P.M.: *Hollywood Babble-On*
The Lovitz, Universal CityWalk

7/18
Tyler Posey, Jeff Davis on
SMorning Show
Jen Schwalbach's House,
Los Angeles
Cinema Enema w/ Jay & Silent
Bob
G4TV, Hollywood

7/19
Holland Roden, Colton Haynes
on SMorning Show
Jen Schwalbach's House,
Los Angeles

7/20
Dylan O'Brien on SMorning
Show
Jen Schwalbach's House,
Los Angeles

7/21
SMeaker Launch/Etnies
Party
Comic-Con International,
San Diego

7/22
Moderate Epix CAPTAINS
panels with William
Shatner
Comic-Con International,
San Diego
8 P.M.: Babble-On Comic-Con
10 P.M.: Jay & Silent Bob Get
Old at Comic-Con
House of Blues, San Diego

7/23
Kev's Annual Hall H Q&A
Comic-Con International,
San Diego

7/26
Kristen Bauer on SMorning
Show
Jen Schwalbach's House, Los
Angeles

7/26–7/27
Test taping for Tonitely pilot
Telepictures, Los Angeles

7/28
SModcast 3D
Montreal Just for Laughs Fest

7/29
Jay & Silent Bob Get Old
The Lovitz, Universal CityWalk

7/30
Hollywood Babble-On
The Lovitz, Universal
CityWalk

AUGUST

8/2
My Birthday

8/3
Red State Podcasters Screening
Laser Pacific, Hollywood

8/4
Matt Jones on SMorning Show
Jen Schwalbach's House,
Los Angeles

8/5
Carol Banker on SMorning
Show
Jen Schwalbach's House,
Los Angeles

8/5
Jay & Silent Bob Get Old
The Lovitz, Universal CityWalk

8/6
Hollywood Babble-On
The Lovitz, Universal CityWalk

8/8
Gary Shandling on *SMorning Show*
Jen Schwalbach's House, Los Angeles

8/10–8/11
Tonitely pilot shoot

8/12
8 P.M.: *Hollywood Babble-On*
10 P.M.: *Jay & Silent Bob Get Old*
Hard Rock Strip, Las Vegas

8/13
8 P.M.: *Hollywood Babble-On*
10 P.M.: *Jay & Silent Bob Get Old Vegas*
Hard Rock Café on the Strip, Las Vegas

8/14
Red Province Tour
Concordia Hall Theater, Montreal

8/15
Red Province Tour
Toronto Underground Cinema, Toronto

8/16
Red Province Tour
Garneau Theater, Edmonton

8/17
Red Province Tour
The Uptown Theater, Calgary

8/18
Red Province Tour
Vogue Theater, Vancouver

8/19
Red State Academy-Qualifying Run
7 P.M.: Screening/Q&A
10 P.M.: Screening/Q&A
New Beverly Cinema, Los Angeles

8/20
Red State Academy-Qualifying Run
7 P.M.: Screening/Q&A
10 P.M.: Screening/Q&A
New Beverly Cinema, Los Angeles

8/21
Red State Academy-Qualifying Run
7 P.M.: Screening/Q&A
10 P.M.: Screening/Q&A
New Beverly Cinema, Los Angeles

8/22
For A Good Time, Call shoot
Red State Academy-Qualifying Run
7 P.M.: Screening/Q&A
10 P.M.: Screening/Q&A
New Beverly Cinema, Los Angeles

8/23
Kevin Pollak on *SMorning Show*
Jen Schwalbach's House, Los Angeles
Red State Academy-Qualifying Run
7 P.M.: Screening/Q&A
10 P.M.: Screening/Q&A
New Beverly Cinema, Los Angeles

8/24
Zac Levi on *SMorning Show*
Jen Schwalbach's House, Los Angeles
Red State Academy-Qualifying Run
7 P.M.: Screening/Q&A
10 P.M.: Screening/Q&A
New Beverly Cinema, Los Angeles

8/26
8 P.M.: *Hollywood Babble-On*
10 P.M.: *Red State* Screening/Q&A
Alamo Drafthouse, San Antonio

8/27
8 P.M.: *Hollywood Babble-On*
10 P.M.: *Red State* Screening/Q&A
Alamo Drafthouse, Houston

8/31
Kelly Carlin on *SMorning Show*
Jen Schwalbach's House, Los Angeles

SEPTEMBER

9/1
Red State hits VOD
AMC greenlights *Secret Stash*
Kev on TMZ
Los Angeles
Tonight Show with Jay Leno
NBC, Burbank
Joe Rogen Experience
Rogen Compound, California

9/2
6 A.M.: TV Satellites for Lionsgate *Red State* VOD release
Los Angeles
10 P.M.: *Jay & Silent Bob Get Old*
The Lovitz, Universal CityWalk

9/3
Hollywood Babble-On
The Lovitz, Universal CityWalk

9/7
Evening with Kevin Smith
Content World Conference
Cleveland, Ohio

9/8
Keynote address, Content World Conference
Cleveland, Ohio

9/9
Eliza Dushku on *SMorning Show*
Jen Schwalbach's House, Los Angeles
Hollywood Babble-On
The Lovitz, Universal CityWalk

9/12
Red State UK Tour
Brixton Ritzy, London

9/13
Red State UK Tour
Cineworld Theaters, Glasgow

9/14
Red State UK Tour
Manchester Odeon, Manchester

9/15
Red State UK
Cineworld Theaters,
   Birmingham

9/16
Plus One London Live
Prince Charles Theater, London

9/25
Red State Streaming Screening/
   Q&A
New Beverly Cinema,
   Los Angeles

9/27
Epix: Kevin Smith Burn in Hell
   shoot
Paramount Theater, Austin

9/29
Rove L.A. taping
Hollywood

9/30
Penn Jillette on *SMorning Show*
Jen Schwalbach's House,
   Los Angeles
8 P.M.: *Jay & Silent Bob Get Old*
10 P.M.: *Hollywood Babble-On*
The Lovitz, Universal CityWalk

OCTOBER

10/4
Craig Brewer on *SMorning
   Show*
Jen Schwalbach's House,
   Los Angeles

10/7
Jay & Silent Bob Get Old
Wilbur Theatre, Boston

10/8
Jay & Silent Bob Get Old
Count Basie, Red Bank

10/14
Jay & Silent Bob Get Old
New York Comic-Con, NYC

10/15
Red State wins Best Picture and
   Best Actor
Sitges Film Festival, Spain
SMoviola: Buckaroo Banzai
Screening/Q&A with
   John Lithgow and Peter
   Weller
Lincoln Center, NYC

10/17
Kev on *The View*
NYC
Hollywood Babble-On
World Café Live, Philadelphia

10/21
Paul Dini & Misty Lee on
   SMorning Show
Jen Schwalbach's House,
   Los Angeles

10/22
Hollywood Babble-On
The Lovitz, Universal
  CityWalk

10/24
Ricky Mabe on *SMorning
  Show*
Jen Schwalbach's House,
  Los Angeles

10/26
Ben Gleib on *SMorning Show*
Jen Schwalbach's House,
  Los Angeles
8 P.M.: *Red State* Screening/
  Q&A
10 P.M.: *Red State* Screening/
  Q&A
The Art Theater, Long Beach

10/27
Twitter Q&A
San Francisco

10/28
8 P.M.: *Jay & Silent Bob Get
  Old*
10 P.M.: *Red State* Screening/
  Q&A
Castro, San Francisco

10/29
Hollywood Babble-On
The Lovitz, Universal CityWalk

NOVEMBER

11/4
Jay & Silent Bob Get Old
Hard Rock Café on the Strip,
  Las Vegas

11/5
Hollywood Babble-On
Hard Rock Café on the Strip,
  Las Vegas

11/7
Evening with Kevin Smith
The Spatz Theater, Halifax,
  Nova Scotia

11/11
Evening with Kevin Smith
Harpa Concert Hall, Reykjavik,
  Iceland

11/13
AMC *Secret Stash* show shoot:
  Podcasting
Red Bank, NJ

11/14
AMC *Secret Stash* show shoot:
  Hockey
Red Bank, NJ

11/15
Stephen Root on *SMorning
  Show*
Jen Schwalbach's House, Los
  Angeles

11/18
Jay & Silent Bob Get Old
Coach House, San Juan
  Capistrano

11/19
Hollywood Babble-On
The Lovitz, Universal CityWalk

11/20
Talking Dead
KCET Studio, Los Angeles

11/21
Harley gets braces

11/22
Jay & Silent Bob Get Old
The Belly-Up, Solana Beach

11/23
Matt Jones and Willful
   Creatures on *SMorning
   Show*
Jen Schwalbach's House,
   Los Angeles

11/26
Hollywood Babble-On
The Lovitz, Universal
   CityWalk

11/30
Paul Scheer, Ben Gleib on
   SMorning Show
Jen Schwalbach's House,
   Los Angeles

DECEMBER

12/2
Jay & Silent Bob Get Old
The Lovitz, Universal CityWalk

12/3
ABC's of SNL
The Lovitz, Universal CityWalk

12/3
Hollywood Babble-On
The Lovitz, Universal CityWalk

12/7
Jay & Silent Bob Get Old
Vogue Theater, Vancouver

12/8
Jay & Silent Bob Get Old
McDougall United Church,
   Edmonton

12/9
Harley's school play
Los Angeles

12/10
Jay & Silent Bob Get Old
The Odeon, Saskatoon

12/11
Jay & Silent Bob Get Old
The Burton Cummings Theater,
   Winnipeg

12/12
Jay & Silent Bob Get Old
The Spatz Theater, Halifax

12/13
AMC *Secret Stash* show shoot:
   Podcasting
Red Bank, NJ

12/14
AMC *Secret Stash* show shoot:
   Podcasting
Red Bank, NJ

12/17
Hollywood Babble-On
The Lovitz, Universal
   CityWalk

12/31
6 P.M.: *Jay & Bob's New Year's
   Eve Poker Classic*
10 P.M.: *New Years Babble-Eve,*
The Lovitz, Universal CityWalk